Learning from teacher research

Edited by John Loughran, Ian Mitchell
and Judie Mitchell

Teachers College
Columbia University
New York and London

Published in the United States by Teachers College Press,
1234 Amsterdam Avenue, New York, NY 10027

Library of Congress Cataloging-in-Publication Data

Learning from teacher research/edited by John Loughran, Ian Mitchell,
and Judie Mitchell
       p. cm.—(Practitioner inquiry series)
    Includes bibliographical references and index
    ISBN 0-8077-4220-1 (pbk).
    1. Education—Research. I. Loughran, J. John. II. Mitchell, Ian J.
    III. Mitchell, Judie. IV. Series
LB1028 L33 2002
370'.7'2—dc21   2001052284

ISBN 0-8077-4220-1 (paper)

09 08 07 06 05 04 03 02   8 7 6 5 4 3 2 1

Contents

Figures and tables

FIGURES

TABLES

Contributors

Amanda Berry taught General Science and Biology for ten years in high schools before joining Monash University as a Science teacher educator. As part of her most recent high school teaching experience, Amanda co-taught Grade 9 and 10 Science classes with her colleague, Philippa Milroy. Through this fulfilling association, Amanda has deepened her interest in and understanding of teaching approaches that promote students' meaningful learning of science concepts.

Lyn Boyle has been a classroom teacher for 20 years. She teaches English, Studies of Society and Education (SOSE) and Psychology. She is currently the Middle Years Coordinator at Newcomb Secondary College, where she established a PEEL group in 1997. She recently completed a certificate in Teaching for Quality Learning and is passionate about the importance of teacher–student relationships established through engaging students in good learning behaviours.

David Burke is currently the Vice-Principal, and a Maths teacher, at Portland Secondary College, located on the south coast of Victoria, about 400 kilometres from Melbourne. He has been teaching for 25 years and has also taught Science and Chemistry. He has been a pioneer in promoting school-wide professional development initiatives in his school with a focus on teaching and learning. David has contributed to three other PEEL/PAVOT books.

Rosemary Dusting is a secondary Mathematics teacher with over fifteen years' experience. She is the co-editor of *Towards a Thinking Classroom: A Study of PEEL Teaching* (PEEL Publishing, Melbourne, 1996). Rosemary was recently seconded to Monash University for two years to lecture in Methods and Practice of Teaching Mathematics to pre-service students. She is now studying for her Masters of Education by research and frequently presents workshops and presentations at Mathematics conferences.

Kerry Fernandez has been teaching English and SOSE in secondary schools for ten years. She has a Masters in Special Education, and has responsibility for special needs English students at Gleneagles Campus of Eumemmerring Secondary College. Kerry's research has radically changed her approach to teaching writing—she now strongly believes in foregrounding the social and communicative aspects of the writing process, and in working with her students in a collaborative relationship.

Jill Flack is a primary teacher with 20 years of teaching experience in a range of educational settings including pre-school, secondary school, university and briefly overseas. Since 1994, Jill has been actively involved in researching her own teaching through the PAVOT project. The process has been an exciting and stimulating professional development experience through which she has been challenged to explore more about what happens and why in her classroom. Jill has taught and worked collaboratively with Jo Osler for many years.

Pia Jeppersen is currently teaching International Baccalaureate Mathematical Studies, IGCSE Extended Mathematics and lower school Mathematics at the New International School of Thailand, in

Bangkok. Prior to this, she taught secondary Mathematics for eight years at the Presbyterian Ladies' College, Melbourne, Australia. Pia has an ongoing interest in developing students' use of linking to promote learning.

Jo Kindred has been teaching for seven years, predominantly in the English, SOSE and Drama areas. She has taken on the roles of Year Level Coordinator and English Coordinator and is currently the Manager of Effective Teaching and Learning at Portland Secondary College. She has been involved in action research for many years and first became interested in the project she conducted with David Burke that led to their chapter in this book when tackling some motivational issues with her Year 9 Journalism class.

John Loughran works in the Faculty of Education at Monash University. He has been actively involved in teacher education for the past decade. His research interests include teacher-as-researcher, reflective practice, science education and teaching and learning. Recent publications include *Developing Reflective Practice, Opening the Classroom Door* (Loughran and Northfield) and *Teaching about Teaching* (Loughran and Russell) (all published by Falmer Press).

Philippa Milroy became a Science (and English) teacher at the age of 30. In her first teaching position, she shared classes with Amanda Berry. This shared venture allowed more risk-taking than either would have attempted alone and gave Philippa an apprenticeship that established teaching for conceptual change as 'normal' in the classroom.

Ian Mitchell is one of the co-founders of the Project for the Enhancement of Effective Learning (PEEL). Ian spent 23 years as a secondary teacher of Chemistry and Mathematics from 1975 to 1997. For fourteen of those years he lectured half-time in the Faculty of Education at Monash University. This long-term dual role provided opportunities for extended classroom research that linked theory and practice. In 1998, Ian accepted a full-time lectureship at Monash and has continued his work through his research interest in teacher knowledge and teacher-as-researcher.

Judie Mitchell has been teaching English for 26 years (Grades 7–12) and since 1995 has been working part-time as project officer for the PAVOT project at Monash University. Judie is a founding member of the PEEL project and has been both a member and convenor of PEEL groups in schools since 1985. Judie's interest in teaching and learning writing is at the heart of her concern for students' learning in English.

Gillian Pinnis is a secondary school teacher with 20 years' experience teaching Psychology, English, History and Geography. She is currently a Year Level Coordinator and has been a Curriculum Coordinator. As a Leader Teacher, she has been responsible for professional development of staff and new educational initiatives. Gillian co-edited *Towards a Thinking Classroom* (PEEL Publishing, Melbourne, 1996) and is currently developing initiatives to aid primary school students in their transition to the secondary school environment.

Jo Osler is a primary teacher whose teaching philosophy has developed through her involvement in the PEEL project. Her work on creating a classroom environment that promotes quality learning is a feature of her teaching. Through her approach to teaching, she has focused on developing students' metacognitive skills. Jo has taught and worked collaboratively with Jill Flack for many years.

Marilyn Smith began her research when she was teaching at Corio Community School, where she taught Grade 11 boys who were at risk of not completing their secondary schooling. Marilyn was also the school's Professional Development Coordinator and from this position was recently promoted to a selective-entry girls' school.

Deborah Tranter is the Assistant Principal at Wheelers Hill Primary School. In her present role, she is also Curriculum Coordinator. The previous four years were spent as the Leading Teacher in Curriculum at The Basin Primary School at the foot of the Dandenong Ranges, where she did her research on homework. Deborah has a deep concern for the quality of her students' learning and this led to the research she has conducted for her chapter in this book.

Meaghan Walsh is a psychologist who has been working in the area of educational psychology research for the past eight years. Her work in both secondary and tertiary education settings has largely focused on assisting students to build independent learning skills, and exploring issues of transition. She currently holds a research position in the Centre for Learning and Teaching in Information Technology, Engineering and Science, at Swinburne University of Technology. Meaghan also works in private practice.

Chris Wilson has been a full-time teacher for 30 years, and has been involved in teacher research for the past seven of those. Through this involvement, and his interest in gifted education, he has explored ways of teaching students better learning skills. This led to his development of an elective called Open Learning that is the focus of his study in this book.

PART 1

Introduction

Teacher as researcher: The PAVOT project

John Loughran

INTRODUCTION

In teaching, there has long been a perceived gap between research and practice. A stereotype that commonly accompanies this perception is that research does not readily inform practice and that the complex and 'messy' world of teaching cannot adequately be theorised by the teachers who are so busy working in that world. Hence, in many ways, it is readily apparent that appropriate research is needed to bridge the world of the theorist and the world of the practitioner by being responsive to the needs and requirements of each.

This tension is embodied in the work of teacher-researchers—practitioners who bring to bear their expert knowledge and understanding of practice *in* their research of *their* practice. Teacher-researchers can be characterised as those practitioners who attempt to better understand their practice, and its impact on their students, by researching the relationship between teaching and learning in their world of work. However, proposing a role of teacher as researcher is not new. Arguments that the teaching role should include a research

3

responsibility have been long and persistent, but the rhetoric has rarely been translated in such a way that the conditions of teachers' work encourage their development as researchers. Stenhouse (1975) was a strong advocate for teacher-researchers, arguing that a research perspective is fundamental to improvement:

> it is difficult to see how teaching can be improved or how curricular proposals can be evaluated without self monitoring on the part of teachers. A research tradition which is accessible to teachers and which feeds teaching must be created if education is to be significantly improved (Stenhouse, 1975, p.165).

Fortunately, teacher research has slowly gained a 'foothold' in the academic literature through the work of advocates such as Lytle and Cochran-Smith (1992), who pushed a strong line of argument about teacher research as a way of knowing. An important aspect of their work was the inherent value in demonstrating that the knowledge base of teaching must inevitably include the teacher's perspective and, in so doing, be drawn from their experiences of their classrooms as that setting is the primary source of knowledge about teaching. It has been through the recognition of the importance of this argument that teacher research has begun to be better valued in the two worlds that have a stake in the nature of teaching and learning—the worlds of theory and practice.

The need for research to be both responsive to, and developed in, the practice setting has been—in part—a catalyst for the PAVOT project (Perspective and Voice of the Teacher) on which the research in this book is based. However, PAVOT had its roots in PEEL (Project for the Enhancement of Effective Learning—see Baird and Mitchell, 1986; Baird and Northfield, 1992), so an understanding of the nature of that project is important for understanding PAVOT and the particulars of its approach to teacher research.

PEEL

In 1984, Science teacher Ian Mitchell, from a school in the western suburbs of Melbourne, Australia, attended a conference presentation by an academic who outlined research he had conducted into the way in which a group of high school students approached learning. In this presentation, Dr John Baird described how he had studied, and consequently classified, students' learning in relation to particular learning behaviours. Baird outlined how his research had highlighted the students' use of Poor Learning Tendencies (see Table 1.1) and how these influenced what and how students do or do not learn.

The impact of this presentation on Mitchell was substantial. He readily identified with Baird's findings as the notion of poor learning tendencies 'rang true' with his experiences of trying to encourage students to take a more active role in learning. From this initial meeting of a teacher and a researcher with a common interest in student learning grew the Project for the Enhancement of Effective Learning (PEEL).

Mitchell presented what he had seen in Baird's research to the staff at his school. He soon realised that a number of his colleagues were already 'primed' in terms of concerns about their students' passive learning, as they similarly identified with Baird's ideas. What was interesting, though, was their ready acceptance of the plan to attempt to tackle these learning difficulties and to support one another in so doing. Through discussion and a genuine interest in pursuing ways of addressing what Baird had uncovered about student learning, the PEEL project was initiated in 1985. The structure that developed included a group of teachers meeting together on a regular basis to discuss their attempts to improve the quality of students' classroom learning. An important aspect of this project was the ongoing involvement of tertiary academics with teachers. However, the academics were not responsible for the organisation or management of the meetings, they were participants, and as such, were both a support and a resource for the teachers. The structure that developed then involved collaboration, support, sharing of ideas and approaches to teaching and, importantly, the development of an articulation of pedagogy through regular meetings in which the discussion of teaching and learning was the central focus.

The PEEL teachers were involved in action research as they collected data, shared their experiences, reflected on the processes

Table 1.1:   Poor Learning Tendencies

1. *Impulsive attention*: patchy attention to the information. Some parts of the information are thought about, other parts are ignored.
2. *Superficial attention*: skimming over or scanning the information, without making an effort to process and understand it.
3. *Inappropriate application*: applying remembered procedures blindly, in the hope that they will give the correct answer.
4. *Inadequate monitoring*: often seen as the learner getting 'stuck' in a problem, and being unable to get 'unstuck' without help.
5. *Premature closure*: not checking to ensure that work done has complied with the task set, leading to an incorrect or inadequate answer.
6. *Ineffective restructuring*: for example, as a result of teaching, a student recognises that he or she has a misconception and comprehends an alternative idea, yet later reverts back to the original misconception.
7. *Lack of reflective thinking*: information learned is in little boxes relatively unrelated to each other.

Source: Baird (1986)

and outcomes and attempted to change the nature of their approach to teaching. Importantly, they documented their experiences, and their first book (Baird and Mitchell, 1986) was (and still is) very well accepted by teachers because it helped to legitimate the efforts associated with the struggle that teachers face as they attempt to improve the quality of their students' learning. This first major PEEL publication, by teachers for teachers, was a starting point for an ever-evolving professional development and research project.

More than a decade after its inception, PEEL continues to grow and develop both nationally and internationally (PEEL groups exist in schools across Australia, as well as in Canada, New Zealand, Sweden and Denmark). Its longevity is exceptional, perhaps due to the fact that the four basic aims of the project are still the driving force for teachers' continued involvement. The aims, as restated in *Learning from the PEEL Experience* (the second major PEEL book: Baird and Northfield, 1992) are to:

Table 1.2:   Some Good Learning Behaviours (GLBs)

Seeks assistance	Tells the teacher what they do not understand
Checks progress	Refers to earlier work before asking for help
Plans work	Anticipates and predicts possible outcomes
Reflects on work	Makes links between activities and ideas
Links ideas and experiences	Offers relevant and personal examples
Develops a view	Justifies opinions

Source: Baird and Northfield (1992)

- foster students' independent learning through training for enhanced metacognition;
- change teachers' attitudes and behaviours to ones that promote such learning;
- investigate processes of teacher and student change as participants engage in action research;
- identify factors that influence successful implementation of a program to improve the quality of classroom learning.

Through PEEL, Baird's research was made accessible to teachers and they identified with it in a way that helped them to actively pursue ways of addressing the inherent difficulties that they could see in their own classrooms. Importantly, PEEL teachers took the notion of poor learning tendencies and turned these into practical ways of developing students' metacognitive skills by developing a list of specific Good Learning Behaviours (GLBs)—behaviours that they could develop with their students to enhance their control over their own learning (see Table 1.2 for a brief list of some GLBs). The list of GLBs has grown over time and has proved to be a 'touchstone for action' for teachers as they have found, through these, ways of addressing their concerns about students' passive learning. They have gained much professional satisfaction in knowing that they have developed (and continue to develop) meaningful ways of enhancing their students' metacognitive skills, which helps facilitate the change from passive to more active, responsible learners.

A crucial aspect of the PEEL project is that it is unfunded. Teachers maintain involvement because they are concerned about the nature and quality of their students' learning and, through PEEL, continue to find ways to both develop their practice and enhance their students' learning. PEEL teachers set the agenda for their exploration of practice and do so in light of their need to develop their students' learning through creative, thoughtful teaching procedures specifically designed to address particular aspects of learning (or non-learning).

Some PEEL teachers became interested in researching their practice in more systematic and organised ways so that what they have learnt about in their classrooms could be shared more widely with others. Thus the PAVOT project, a teacher research project driven by the research concerns of PEEL teachers, was initiated.

THE PERSPECTIVE AND VOICE OF THE TEACHER (PAVOT) PROJECT

PAVOT began in 1994 as an (unfunded) offspring of PEEL that offered an opportunity for teachers to collaborate more closely with academic supporters in more systematic research. As was the case with PEEL, the research was to be led and controlled by the teachers. From 1995, PAVOT has twice been funded by the Australian Research Council (ARC) through two three-year Large Grants. These ARC Large Grants were specifically designed to research teacher learning through the application of PEEL teaching across a variety of school settings. PAVOT is now at the end of its second three years of funding (this important ARC support also illustrates the shift in the research focus discussed in the introduction to this chapter) and continues to attract teachers who are interested in researching their own classrooms and teaching practice.

PAVOT was specifically set up to:

> assist teachers to research aspects of their practice. It is a natural extension of PEEL in that it aims to support teachers in documenting and communicating the kind of teaching and learning

that occurs with active involvement in PEEL, and to further explore issues which are important to teachers in their daily work (Mitchell and Mitchell, 1997, p. 3).

Therefore PAVOT has given teachers opportunities to develop their individual voices and to document and portray their research findings — and thus to share their pedagogical knowledge with other educationalists. PAVOT is an overt example of valuing teacher research, and the fact that it has attracted ARC funding is testament to the education community's recognition both of the value and importance of such work and that the knowledge about teaching genuinely resides with teachers—but needs support if it is to be better recognised and portrayed for others. The funding, however, has not been used to 'pay' teachers to conduct research, or to 'buy them out' of existing teaching responsibilities. Rather, it has been used to develop ways of supporting teacher research through creating opportunities for teachers to access short-term classroom release (Casual Relief Teacher funding for such things as writing days, PAVOT meetings, etc.) and funding for teachers to present their research findings at educational conferences (travel and other incidental costs both nationally—Australasian Science Education Research Association conference, Australian Association for Research in Education conference—and internationally—American Education Research Association conference, International Conference for Teacher Researchers), as well as for ongoing collaboration with other teacher-researchers and academics.

Schön's (1983, 1987) notion of reframing the problematic situation is one way of conceptualising teachers' desire to be involved in PAVOT. Teacher-researchers have begun to 'look into' their classrooms in different ways and to seek data that might shed new light on their teaching and their students' learning. This reframing has been facilitated through the work of PEEL and the development of a set of principles (Mitchell and Mitchell, 1997) about the nature of quality teaching derived from years of reflection on practice with and by PEEL teachers. These Principles of Teaching for Quality Learning (see Table 1.3) have been useful in creating a language that has helped to give meaning to 'what it is' that can be problematic in teaching while at the same time creating 'ways in' for examining teaching and learning situations.

Table 1.3:   Principles of Teaching for Quality Learning

1. Share intellectual control with students.
2. Look for occasions when students can work out part (or all) of the content or instructions.
3. Provide opportunities for choice and independent decision-making.
4. Provide a diverse range of ways of experiencing success.
5. Promote talk that is exploratory, tentative and hypothetical.
6. Encourage students to learn from other students' questions and comments.
7. Build a classroom environment that supports risk-taking.
8. Use a wide variety of intellectually challenging teaching procedures.
9. Use teaching procedures that are designed to promote specific aspects of quality learning.
10. Develop students' awareness of the big picture: how the various activities fit together and link to the big ideas
11. Regularly raise students' awareness of the nature of components of quality learning.
12. Promote assessment as part of the learning process.

TEACHER RESEARCH FOR PERSONAL UNDERSTANDING

Another aspect of reframing has involved reframing the nature of the research itself—and thus viewing research as problematic. By looking into the classroom through a teacher-researcher lens, it is not difficult to recognise that, generally, their approach to research and the manner in which they report their findings is different to that of 'traditional' educational researchers because it is largely driven by a personal imperative—wanting to make a difference for their students. Therefore, just as Dewey (1929) noted so long ago, educational practices themselves must be the source of the ultimate problems to be investigated if we are to build a science of education, so a focus on teacher research is paramount as it is teachers who work in the crucible of educational practice from which the 'problems' are derived. Clearly, then, the point of this focus on teacher research is that the results of such investigations should inform the practice setting—and its practitioners—and therefore begin to address the theory–practice gap that is so often cited as a barrier to progression in teaching and learning. We trust that the examples of teacher research in this book offer some insights into the nature of teacher research and some of the valuable outcomes of teacher research.

Another important aspect of the teacher-researchers involved in PAVOT is that, beyond not being 'employed' to be teacher-researchers (all their research is additional to their normal school teaching duties and workloads), they are in fact volunteers who choose to examine their practice and their students' learning for the inherent benefits of such action to their professional practice. Furthermore, none of these teacher-researchers was involved in research as part of a postgraduate award—although a couple have been encouraged to pursue 'academic credit' for their work as a consequence of their later involvement in postgraduate studies. Therefore, the value of teacher research to the individual practitioner is further highlighted by the very fact that they choose to be involved in projects that are not created for a substantial external reward.

The chapters in this book, then, illustrate how some of the teacher-researchers involved in PAVOT have developed their research agendas, and their accounts offer a range of valuable insights into the nature of teaching, learning and research.

REPORTING TEACHER RESEARCH

All of the teacher-researchers who have contributed to this book have had ongoing involvement in PEEL and PAVOT. This book is an example of the type of research that teachers choose to conduct as they come to confront issues and concerns in their own practice. These chapters also shed light on the nature of these teachers' particular research needs and offer a range of approaches to, and ways of seeing, teaching and learning.

In completing this research, each author constructed a substantial draft of their chapter before meeting together to discuss their work. They reviewed one another's studies in small groups and offered feedback. This was done by considering how clearly their work addressed each of the following questions:

1. *Context:* What is the study about and why—how is it of interest to you in your work?
2. *Research question/s:* What are you trying to find the answer to and why?
3. *Method:* What did you do and how, who was involved, when did they do it, how often, where do they come from (parents, students, etc.); is this written in such a way that someone else could replicate your study by using your interview questions, surveys, discussions, etc.?
4. *Results:* What did you find out and what are those findings based on—what are the major thematic sub-headings of your work?
5. *What you have learnt:* What did all of this mean to you and your teaching/research?
6. *Conclusion:* What do you think it all means and why does it matter?

Following these sessions, each of the teacher-researchers revisited the draft of their report to take into account the feedback they had received. Their final drafts then became the basis for this book. At the end of the process (when the first full draft of the book was completed), the teams all met together again to consider the insights that they had gained about teacher research as a result of reading all the work.

The book is organised into parts based around some of the themes that emerged through the communication of the research, but is not limited to these—this is only one way of viewing the work. Hence the three parts that we have used to conceptualise the presentation of these PAVOT teachers' research are designed to highlight the systematic and organised nature of their approach to research while maintaining (as much as possible) the complexity of their work. These chapters offer a rich range of types of teacher research through the diversity of:

• data (e.g. critical incidents, changes in students' learning behaviours, students' voice, details about changes in teaching);

- problems (e.g. students' passive learning, approaches to teaching, construction and value of teacher knowledge);
- approaches (e.g. collaborative, responding to students' views/attitudes, reflecting on extensive experiences);
- insights (e.g. better articulating the relationship between teaching and learning, the nature of the process of teacher-research, teacher change); and,
- advice for others (e.g. about changes in teaching/students' learning, context-specific advice on teaching and learning).

In Part 2, 'Researching Changes in Teaching', developing a better understanding of teaching and some of the influences on teaching were the catalysts for researching practice. The complexity of this categorisation is perhaps most evident in Chapter 5, in which the relationship between teaching and learning is constantly evident, yet the main focus is how student learning influenced and caused changes in the teaching approach(es). This Part then highlights how different approaches to data collection, the importance of addressing 'taken for granted' aspects of practice and the need to be responsive to the changes in the way research projects develop influence the way these teacher-researchers pursue their research questions. However, these aspects are not limited to this section but are perhaps highlighted further by the teacher's ability to 'fit research in' to the daily life of schooling (Loughran and Northfield, 1996) so that it can be grasped and examined. This section may then be an example of *teacher research as practical inquiry* as it could well be argued that these projects are concerned with, 'enhanc[ing] immediate classroom change and to provide insight into professional practice . . . [as they] respond to the immediacy of the knowledge needs [these] teachers confront in everyday practice (Cochran-Smith and Lytle, 1999, p. 19). Yet to simply 'categorise' these studies this way is also limiting for there is little doubt that, based on the data sources from which their evidence is sought, their concern to see beyond their particular participant biases is not only clear, but explicitly challenged in the way they test their claims with valued others and/or against their initial findings and conclusions.

Part 3, 'Researching Changes in Learning', illustrates how, for these teachers, the language of learning which has developed and extended through involvement in PEEL and PAVOT has offered new ways of understanding both student learning and, more importantly, how that is specifically linked to teachers' approaches and purposes in teaching. These chapters extend the notion of 'teaching against the grain' (Cochran-Smith, 1991) for these authors' purpose in doing this is directly linked to a need to effect change in students' understanding of, and approaches to, learning (an issue that also underpins Part 4 of the book). Interestingly though—an intriguing element of the reference base that many of these teacher-researchers in this book call upon—is that their work is largely internally referenced through their knowledge and understanding of PEEL. This raises questions that challenge some of the perspectives offered as critiques of teacher research (Cochran-Smith and Lytle, 1999). For example: 'Is there an accessible and coherent international literature base of teacher research?'; and 'Is it reasonable to expect that teacher-researchers would draw on a range of literature when it is widely acknowledged that reading is not "normal" for teachers?' In this case, the internal literature has been important. However, the personal knowledge of the work of others (from PEEL and PAVOT), and the ability to learn from and with these people, as they have extended their ideas and research by taking the dilemmas and issues generated from one project and pursued them further in different contexts, was perhaps more important. Knowledge of colleagues' practice combined with ongoing discussion has always been important to teachers. PEEL and PAVOT have been informative and therefore supportive for teacher-researchers in enabling them to better understand the processes associated with their examinations of the uncertainties associated with challenging views and practices of learning.

Part 4, 'Learning Through Reflective Practice', is essentially a window into the complex and protracted journey that teacher-researchers embark upon and learn through. Through critical reflection (Brookfield, 1995), these chapters illustrate that it is not really possible to separate the process from the product and that, in truly coming to understand the changes that have taken place (learning from their findings), there is an explicit need to share the wisdom they have gained—and they share it in most engaging and creative ways.

These chapters are compelling accounts of the growth and development of teacher-researchers, and they highlight the value of linking practice to research so that research informs practice. More particularly, they hint at the transformative possiblities of teacher research on university culture (Cochran-Smith and Lytle, 1999) for the insights into teachers and teaching illuminated through these chapters are not confined to 'school teachers'. Reflective practice is a critical component of practice in any setting. These authors illustrate the value of reflection in confronting dilemmas and of pursuing an understanding of one's own growth and development over time through a serious regard for learning about practice.

VALUING TEACHER RESEARCH

This book offers interesting ways of viewing questions such as: 'What evidence do these teachers rely upon to make decisions about their practice?'; 'To what extent do these teachers theorise?'; and 'How does systematic data collection and writing impact on the need to produce evidence that is convincing to oneself and to others?' There is little doubt that these teacher-researchers show a concern for evidence. For them, the evidence must initially be compelling first to themselves; then, through reporting and communicating their findings, it must also be credible and valid to other teachers; and finally it must perhaps strike a chord with other audiences such as academics.

As Jeff Northfield, a valued colleague and long-time supporter of teacher-researchers, has argued, there is a need for teacher-researchers to accept the 'authority of [their own] experience' (Munby and Russell, 1994). Authority of experience can be seen as an encouragement to teachers to place more faith in their own experience and knowledge, which in turn can help them to meet their own expectations of 'what counts' in teacher research. For many, this may well be preferable to relying more on 'external solutions' that are often problematic in themselves, especially if one considers that it is not uncommon for teacher knowledge to be dismissed (by both educational researchers and, sadly, by teachers) as anecdotal and of little value compared with more traditional forms of research knowledge.

If a recognition of the authority of experience is grasped, then teacher research can be better understood as a form of participant research that brings with it different research demands and dilemmas from traditional research. Teacher research has unique features that need to be recognised and acknowledged because, for these researchers, the tension is not of purpose or of conduct, but one of time and task.

> My research efforts were most often compatible with—and enhanced—my teaching ... My initial purpose for keeping a journal was to document classroom events and my reactions to them so I would have a daily record of my research experience. However, I soon realized that dictating entries on my drive home from school each day had an immediate, positive impact on my teaching ... Had I not been conducting classroom research, I probably would not have kept a journal and thus would not have been as thoughtful about what was working and was not working in my teaching ... The research process, therefore, was compatible with my teaching ... If we begin to think of teacher research as its own genre and teacher researchers as methodologists trying to solve vexing logistical and philosophical problems in classroom inquiry, conflicts or tensions become a natural, if not healthy, aspect of the research evolutionary process (Baumann, 1996, pp. 31–32, 34).

Being a teacher-researcher illustrates professionalism in terms of a willingness to accept that one's own experience is the major source of improvement in practice. However, this is not to suggest that it should be viewed as an individual and isolated activity, for the process of teacher research is enhanced if it is a collaborative venture. When teachers meet to share their knowledge and understanding about teaching and learning, they share their concerns and respond readily to each other's ideas. They develop tentative theories, and the notion of 'practical enquiry' (Richardson, 1994) may well describe teachers using a research process primarily for improving their own practice rather than for communication and publication to a wider audience. However, through PAVOT, some groups of teachers have grasped the opportunity to be engaged in research efforts that go beyond this notion, whereby they have focused on studying specific concerns, discussing interventions, identifying ways of collecting and analysing data, and accepting responsibility for communicating their knowledge and understanding to wider audiences. In many ways, such teachers can therefore be characterised as examining their own developing knowledge base and accepting the professional responsibilities that accompany such a decision, thus highlighting the importance to the educational community of better understanding and valuing teacher research.

I trust that you find the teacher research reported in this book to be a compelling argument for placing greater emphasis on this approach to better understanding teaching and learning. I have no doubt that these chapters will further highlight the importance and value of focusing on the issues, concerns and dilemmas that teachers face in their own classrooms. It is therefore crucial that the research into these issues, concerns and dilemmas be conducted *by* teachers as *they* are also the important *users* of the knowledge gained through such valuable work.

REFERENCES

Baird, J.R. (1986). Learning and Teaching: The Need for Change. In J.R. Baird and I.J. Mitchell (eds) *Improving the Quality of Teaching and Learning: An Australian Case Study—the PEEL Project.* Melbourne: Monash University.

Baird, J.R. and Mitchell, I.J. (1986). *Improving the Quality of Teaching and Learning: An Australian Case Study—the PEEL Project.* Melbourne: Monash University.

Baird, J.R. and Northfield, J.R. (1992). *Learning from the PEEL Experience.* Melbourne: Monash University.

Baumann, J.F. (1996). Conflict or Compatibility in Classroom Inquiry? One teacher's struggle to balance teaching and research. *Educational Researcher* 25 (7), 29–36.

Brookfield, S.D. (1995). *Becoming a Critically Reflective Teacher.* San Francisco: Jossey-Bass.

Cochran-Smith, M. (1991). Learning to Teach Against the Grain. *Harvard Educational Review*, 51 (3), 279–310.

Cochran-Smith, M. and Lytle, S.L. (1999). The Teacher Research Movement: A Decade Later. *Educational Researcher*, 28 (7), 15–25.

Dewey, J. (1929). *The Sources for a Science of Education*. New York: Liveright.

Lytle, S.L. and Cochran-Smith, J. (1992). Teacher Research as a Way of Knowing. *Harvard Educational Review*, 62 (4), 447–74.

Loughran, J.J. and Northfield, J.R. (1996). *Opening the Classroom Door: Teacher, Researcher, Learner*. London: Falmer Press.

Mitchell, I.J. and Mitchell, J.A., (eds) (1997). *Stories of Reflective Teaching: A Book of PEEL Cases*. Melbourne: PEEL Publishing.

Munby, H. and Russell, T. (1994). The Authority of Experience in Learning to Teach: Messages from a Physics Method Class. *Journal of Teacher Education*, 45 (2), 86–95.

Richardson, V. (1994). Conducting Research on Practice. *Educational Researcher*, 23 (5), 5–10.

Schön, D.A. (1983). *The Reflective Practitioner: How Professionals Think in Action*. New York: Basic Books.

—— (1987). *Educating the Reflective Practitioner: Toward a New Design for Teaching and Learning in the Professions*. San Francisco: Jossey-Bass.

Stenhouse, L. (1975). *An Introduction to Curriculum Research and Development*. London: Heinemann.

Wilson, S.M. (1995). Not Tension but Intention: A Response to Wong's Analysis of the Researcher/Teacher. *Educational Researcher* 24 (8), 19–22.

PART 2

Researching changes in teaching

2

Choices and voices: Students take control of their writing

Kerry Fernandez and Judie Mitchell

CONTEXT

This story has a number of characters. The characters in this multi-vocal text are the 25 students of 7B; the English teacher/observer, Kerry Fernandez; and Judie Mitchell, a colleague and observer. It is the combination of the voices that produces the narrative and the story is incomplete and inconclusive if any one voice is dominant or omitted. We have chosen to tell this story as a narrative, in our own voices. A complexity of perspectives is evident in the different individual experiences of the 25 students of 7B (Year 7 being the first year of high school). These students had been together as a class for approximately six months when this series of writing lessons began. They came from various primary schools, both government and Catholic, within the local area.

We collected data in a variety of ways: student surveys, student texts, audio taped interviews and the field notes made by Judie as she viewed and interacted with the students. There were also observations and notes made by myself as 7B's English teacher. Our data were collected over a semester. A video was also made of a discussion session conducted twelve months after our data collection began. This discussion lesson involved inviting the students to articulate how much they remembered about the writing processes that they had been involved in twelve months previously, and their feelings about that experience.

KERRY

I believe that writing is a form of communication that is complex and requires the formulation of ideas and the sharing of meaning. Within a school setting, however, writing is often performed as an isolated act. Students are provided with a topic or choose a topic, and mostly have to write on their own. Treating writing as an isolating task, detached from a social process, fundamentally alters the nature of writing as a communicative act.

I had become intrigued by the theoretical concept of metacognition. White (1988) theorised memory as having seven elements. There are two elements of this model that are pertinent to this story—an *episode* (a memory of an event one took part in or witnessed) and *cognitive strategies* (general skills involved in controlling thinking). One of my guiding themes was to alter students' perceptions of school writing by creating a positive episode, or succession of episodes. The proposition I began with was: could an atmosphere be created that would encourage students to be enjoyably involved in the construction of their own texts? I wondered if I could create an episode which the students would not only remember, but which would alter their negative attitudes to school writing. In terms of cognitive strategies, I wanted students to become more aware of the processes involved in the construction of their own writing. If they possessed an explicit understanding of these processes, they would be in a position to have greater control over the construction of their own texts. I was also inviting them to be more in control of their own thinking.

The story has its origins in the impromptu—not the unplanned, but the unexpected. As 7B's English teacher, I had arranged with Judie that she would observe a lesson in which we would find out more about 'how students feel about writing'. However, I had forgotten this arrangement until I sighted Judie heading towards 7B's classroom. The lesson for the day was shelved and hastily a forum for discussion took its place. The statement 'thrown' at the students was: 'Put your hand up if you like writing.' When I was bombarded with an overwhelmingly negative rejoinder, I realised I was going to have to be adaptable.

In that first impromptu lesson, there were only four students who claimed to like writing. Their reasons were:

I like writing when I can think of something good for a story.

When something bad happens to me I like to write about it happening to someone else.

I used to have good ideas but now I don't. I think it's because I don't read as much as I used to.

I find writing easy. I can always come up with some ideas. I enjoy writing.

When the statement was reversed, however, a cacophony of voices rose round the classroom. For several minutes, the students were given the unfettered freedom to express their dissatisfaction with writing. The most common cry was that writing was BORING! They were asked to elaborate on this explanation:

Last year in Grade 6 we had to do an hour and a half every day and we got sick of it.

I can never think of the next sentence.

It's not fun and we could be doing other things.

If I need help, I have to wait for the teacher. I had to keep my hand up and my arm got sore.

I would do a movie or a play.

In Grade 3 we had to do an hour and a half of writing each day.

We were not allowed to use the names of the people in the grade, which spoiled the story because it was more interesting to include real people in the story.

We weren't allowed to write mean things about a real person without asking their permission and they always said 'no'.

It's better if we could write at home.

The pen runs out. It's also waste of paper when you have to do drafts.

Evan stated in all seriousness that he just didn't have any imagination. Katherine's comment is particularly pertinent: 'Maybe stories are boring because the writer wants them to be boring.' Another way of construing this comment is to rephrase it. When there is little or no incentive to write, is there a lack of intrinsic motivation? As such, does the act of writing become boring?

Judie and I recorded the students' concerns and then threw the discussion back to them. What would make writing more enjoyable? They talked amongst themselves and then wrote down their comments and shared them with great enthusiasm. It is important to display the wide range of their recommendations:

Make it more interesting by not including any boring or slow parts if it's supposed to be an adventure story. Otherwise the reader thinks it's going to be like that for the whole story.

Put more problems in it, more adventure, more mystery, make it funny. Make bad things happen if you are angry.

More action, more Spice Girls, less drafts.

Write stories in a group. Do just one copy. It helps knowing it will get somewhere. Make it into a play, a film or a book.

Include whoever you want. Write in your own time span.

Include real people. Make it something that you would want to read.

No romance or love bits.

Choose what kind of story we wanted to write. Talk about it instead of just writing about it. Choose which people we want to be in it. Write in a group.

Write a story based on your own hobbies.

Tell people what to write instead of having to write it yourself. Not so many drafts. You forget what you are about to write if you have a long sentence to write. Tape it so that we could look at it. Use other people's names.

Write about people in your grade or school. Write about famous people.

Write any words or things you want. Write a story with your friends so that it has different ideas in it.

Write about any subject you want and you could swear in it to express your feelings.

Only write for half an hour at a time.

Not so many rough copies. Choose what kind of story we want to write.

Make it into a video, a play or a book. Talk about it instead of writing about it.

The students of 7B certainly had their own definite views on the way in which the construction of their own texts should take place.

JUDIE

I saw three main areas of student complaint. The first was the individualistic nature of the writing they had to do. Secondly, they felt they had to write too much and too often. Thirdly, they wanted more control over their texts—what form they would take, the language they used and who and what could be included.

There was a clear plea from the students to let them write together in a social situation. One of the main concerns for students is that they are generally expected to write in isolation. During a later data collection session, Cara said about most of her school writing: 'The silence deafens you.' (June 1999)

Crowley points out the social nature of language:

> The solitude that often accompanies the act of writing seduces writers into believing they are engaged in individual acts of creation; it is all too easy to forget, while writing, that one's language belongs to a community of speakers and writers, that one has begun writing in order to reach (absent) readers, and that one's 'innovative ideas' have long textual histories behind them, histories which contain many voices (Crowley, 1989, p. 35).

Language *is* communication, and expecting students to write what is ostensibly a piece of communication without discussing it seems unnatural and cruel to them. They believe they cannot get good ideas unless they talk together.

KERRY

Through listening to the voices of these young writers, I was provided with a different perspective by which to plan future lessons. I developed a unit of loosely constructed lesson plans that incorporated the students' ideas. I was prepared to take the risk of following the direction of the students. This proved to be a decisive turning point in my own appreciation of the way in which texts are constructed.

In the next lesson, I put forward a scheme that would meet the needs of the students and asked for their feedback. I explained to the class about the boundaries within which I, as their English teacher, had to operate—such as curriculum and appropriate language. The only boundaries that were fixed were those of genre and censorship of language. Prior to the commencement of these writing sessions, 7B had studied the genre of adventure through the film *Indiana Jones and the Last Crusade*. Thus they were required to display their understanding of the aspects of this genre in their own writing.

Apart from these two restrictions, the students had total control over what kinds of texts they wrote and how they wrote them. Predictably, all but one of them chose to work in groups, ranging in size from two to eight. The formation of their writing groups was very much along lines of gender and level of social development. The largest writing collective was a 'socially aware' group whose play was set very much in the modern era. This collective consisted of Sam, Claire, Steven, Sharyn, Mark, Marie, David and Ewan. Another large group was made up of girls: Shae, Kate, Bree, Yvonne, Belinda, Kirsty and Kathy. The way in which they adapted the genre of adventure was to align it to fantasy. Correspondingly there was an all-boys group: Adam, Tony, Kevin, Bobby and Erik. They chose the Western adventure. They also co-opted the services of a girl to play the supplicant female who could be 'saved'. Sean chose to write an adventure story by himself. David K. and Alan elected to present their story in cartoon form. Mark L. and Darrell wrote an adventure story set in the future.

Having selected their own groupings, the following lessons were highly productive. They wrote practically nothing! However, what was achieved was a total immersion in communication. Essentially what they were being asked to do was to solve a problem. The problem was to construct an adventure text. They used problem-solving communicative techniques to achieve this end. Garton and Pratt point out that: 'In social interaction, children learn to use the tools that will enable them to achieve the ends or goals they require.' (Garton and Pratt, 1989, p. 41). Prior to writing, they discussed, they play-acted, they debated and argued, until a resolution was achieved by the group.

A theoretical perspective that is applicable to the way in which these young people were seen to interact is Vygotsky's (1986) social interactionist theory. This theory pertains to the way in which individuals relate mutually to produce an effective communication, by voice, gesture and facial expression. This theory has its basis in human social development. As individuals interact, social practices are learned, communication is shared and meaning is developed. When the students of 7B chose their groups for this series of writing sessions, they formed into social groups which suited their various stages of social development. There was already the basis of social interaction present.

The writing sessions took place during one period per week over the second semester and culminated in the videotaping of the performance pieces, the reading of the stories and the displaying of the cartoons. This time frame allowed other areas of the English curriculum to be addressed.

The writing sessions were a period of time to be looked forward to. While I was preoccupied with overseeing the class, Judie observed and took field notes. She not only recorded observations of student interaction but also spoke with them, gaining their opinions of how they were viewing the writing lessons.

JUDIE

The task overcame all three of the students' objections to writing. They worked in social groups as a community of speakers and writers, sharing their voices and ideas. The resulting student texts were rich and vibrant—illustrating vividly the extensive textual histories these students already possessed, at the ages of 12 and 13. Their texts were full of, but not derivative of, the adventure films they had seen, the TV shows they had watched and the video games they played.

Working in groups also reduced the amount of actual writing they each had to do. The drafting process took care of itself in the conversation (and also in the acting out and the amassing of props and costumes). Their arms and hands did not get sore!

The choice of plays by so many groups may have helped them meet their need to use their peers as models for characters. Teachers know the ways in which children can deliberately hurt each other in their writing. As Gee (1996) says, words can be 'loaded weapons'. However, most authors use their real-life friends and relations in some way in creating their characters in novels and plays. Creating a character based on a person who is then acted by another person puts a distance between the words and the person who was the original inspiration.

Having control over the form of text, the language and the content allowed them much more creativity. They were (surprisingly) purposeful and deliberate about the choices they made about what sort of language to include, and how they would use their peers as models for characters. I observed in my field notes:

> Groups are all working and so ON TASK! When I came over to the girls' group they were sitting around writing the script (for their fantasy adventure play). After about fifteen minutes they were up and acting it out. It seemed such a spontaneous move to do this.
>
> The boys' group (Western adventure play) has a huge bag of props: guns, hats, etc. They enter into negotiation with Kerry about using caps [blanks] (in the guns).

It surprised me that, given the opportunity, the majority of students began immediately to think of their writing in terms of much more than simply words on a page. Allowed to work with their friends and to write drama, they launched themselves into writing that was more in line with Gee's idea of 'Discourse' than the usual 'discourse' of school writing:

> I will use the word discourse for connected stretches of language that make sense, like conversations, stories, reports, arguments, essays and so forth. So 'discourse' is part of 'Discourse'.

> Discourses are ways of being in the world, or forms of life which integrate words, acts, values, beliefs and social identities, as well as gestures, glances, body positions and clothes. A discourse is a sort of social identity kit which comes complete with the appropriate costume and instructions on how to act, talk and often write, so as to take on a particular social role that others will recognize (Gee, 1996, p. 127).

One girl wanted to build a wedding into the group's story because she had a wedding dress at home she wanted to wear. Another student said:

> it was fun watching everyone . . . trying to be their characters, like some people didn't fit their character but they are now.

The all-girls group wrote a play they called 'Old':

> Our play is quite old and all that, and we had to get the names that matched the oldness of it, like Maudula. Shae made us write old English things like, instead of saying thank you, she's got to say much obliged.

They chose not to use swear words because the language (swearing) was not the 'proper form'.

The all-boys group found that collecting props helped them visualise and conceptualise the kind of story they would write. The boys who did the cartoon could express their ideas visually, with a minimum of text.

The idea of discourse and Discourse also played out in the groups they chose. The mixed-gender group considered themselves socially superior to the other students and membership of this group was strictly controlled. They said they enjoyed working as a group because they could choose their friends and were 'not hanging around with the geeks'. The shy boys chose to work in pairs, and the other two groups were single-sex groups.

KERRY

An interesting feature of the writing lessons was that the students began to see me not as their English teacher, not as the person who gave specific directives but as someone whom they could use as a reference point. When they were satisfied with a particular section of their text, they would excitedly ask me to view it or read it. Their self/group editing had eliminated many of the structural errors that so often plague student writing—spelling, punctuation, sentence structure, etc.

What I observed was groups of young people using speech and other ways of communicating to organise their collective ideas. In their groups, they were transferring their ideas into written language in a very personally meaningful way.

WAS AN EPISODE CREATED?
DID IT CHANGE THEIR VIEWS?

Kerry and Judie

Twelve months after this writing episode, members of the class were invited to discuss what they remembered of it. The class discussion was videotaped. The data collected indicated that an episode was created, but it did not change their views about writing. It appeared to us that one episode, albeit a long one, was not enough to impact on these students' memories of years of boring school writing tasks.

They remembered vividly many aspects of the writing episode. The context of the discussion was interesting too—when Kerry asked them to move into the groups they had been in for the writing, they did so immediately and animatedly, even though there had been a number of changes in the class; some students were no longer present, and some had not been there in 1998.

They remembered that being able to 'use language' (by which they meant negotiated swear words) made their writing 'more fun', 'more real'. When asked what lines they remembered, each group could remember easily some significant lines. It may be true that, being mostly plays, the lines stuck, but the groups who wrote the cartoon and the story also remembered lines. These lines show the quality of the writing, and their understanding of the rules of the adventure genre. The story group remembered their opening lines, a conversation:

I've done it! I've done it!

You've done what?

I've created a time machine!

The boys who did the cartoon remembered one of their speech bubbles:

I've got some special powers.

The boys with the guns remembered the action scene in the bar:

You're gonna die Jake, you're gonna die!

I don't think so!

Members of the socially advanced group proudly quoted two lines which they clearly treasured, from the expression they managed to instil into them. And of course it is difficult to convey this expression in writing—a point which seems to underlie much of this paper's argument. They also insisted on putting the lines into the context:

You are an uni*mag*inable bastard.

When Ewan asked me for a kiss, I said, 'If I was a fly I wouldn't land in your shit any day!'

They loved being able to work in groups and to move around: 'We didn't have to sit at a table all day'. They loved having choices, not having to do individual drafts, and that they got to talk to their friends and didn't have to be quiet. They appreciated working in friendship groups because 'we knew what each other was like'. One student stated that it was the 'first *real* story that we've been writing'. They remembered who had what parts in the plays, being able to play with their props, act out their roles, and 'use our voices'.

One group, however, had more negative memories. For them the episode made them 'hate writing even more, 'cos we couldn't agree on some things'. They commented that they:

> would only add two lines and she'd take it home and write six pages, and we'd have to agree to it otherwise she'd threaten to pull out of the group.

Kerry observed that the girl in question (who had now left the school so was not present during this lesson) was a gifted writer. However, her peers were not impressed with the final results—they said the story was too slow, and not interesting enough. They also described the girl in an interview as being 'a control freak'.

The mixed-sex group also had disagreements over the content of their play. In the interview this exchange took place:

> The girls wanted one thing and the boys wanted another.

> The boys wanted to, like, have all fighting and that.

> Yeah, they wanted to be heroes and be fantastic and us girls wanted to . . .

> Yeah, but they wanted to get married . . .

> And have a crash in a limousine . . .

We asked them then whether they had changed their ideas about writing. Their comments were a depressing repetition of the comments from twelve months earlier. In trying to probe why this might be, it seemed that they regarded this episode as too different from their usual school writing.

It wasn't just like writing, it was drama too.

It was a different sort of writing—that's why it was fun.

Their comments are a major concern to us as English teachers. They commented on the amount of theory they had to write in other subjects (copying from the board or from books), the emphasis on spelling, the isolation of it all ('we don't do group work', 'we have to think of all the ideas ourselves', 'our friends can't help us'), the uncomfortable seats, the tired arms and hands from so many drafts.

Judie

Much of the individualisation of writing in schools is driven by assessment—as teachers, we don't always want the hassles of dealing with group problems and ascertaining which student has contributed what to a group project. The outcomes-driven nature of the state's [Victoria's] curriculum documents force us into these positions as well—we are forced into reporting on whether Cindy in Year 8 can individually measure up to a certain standard. We are forced to put into the background other important skills that Cindy may have, such as being willing to collaborate and share ideas with her peers, and mentoring a less able friend in the art of spelling. In the final two years of secondary schooling, we are constrained by the apparent necessity of 'authentication'—the need to be 'certain' it is the student's own work. We need to interrogate more critically our objections to group work, and collaborative writing. Crowley (1989) presents us with:

> the notion recently advanced by some composition theorists that all writing is collaborative. Research into the production of writing in the marketplace has established that most of this sort of writing is the product of many hands (1989, p. 37).

Not only is much writing beyond school collaborative, but it also has a defined purpose, a target audience and results in terms of clear (good or bad) consequences. When we interrogate most school writing using these criteria, it is easy to see why many students find school writing meaningless and boring.

The episode Kerry provided for the students of 7B involved considerable risks. It would have been much easier for her and her mental health to have forced the students to write individual stories seated at their desks in silence. They would have hated it but they would have done it (without much of a murmur, because they are rarely asked for their opinions). Instead, Kerry found herself with a bunch of noisy, active Year 7 students, who repeatedly tested the boundaries of what was and was not 'allowed'. She needed to be flexible in her timing; she could not put arbitrary time frames on this task—as she says, it was a problem-solving exercise and any artificial time frame would destroy the 'scientific method'. This meant other aspects of the curriculum had to be ignored or put aside. The fact that they chose to write plays meant organising and stage managing a dramatic space and a major performance.

The students appreciated Kerry's efforts. They noted that:

> You learn more if there is not so many boundaries. If you've got so many boundaries, like you can't do this and you can't do that, then you can't experience more things so you don't learn more things.

> When you're acting it out, I think it is better than writing, because then you know if something is wrong, and it doesn't fit in, like in the hill part . . .

Kerry

In this research, I radically changed my approach to teaching writing. I handed over almost complete control to the students (Year 7) over what and how they would write. Through my observations of students constructing their own texts and by listening to the voices of the students, my own preconceived notions of writing were challenged. Over a period of time, I began to see myself, during these writing sessions, not as the 'teacher' but more as the resource person whom students could access when the need arose. The students became more reliant upon themselves and their peers in terms of solving their writing problems.

REFERENCES

Crowley, R. (1989). *A Teacher's Introduction to Deconstruction*. Urbana, Illinois: National Council of Teachers of English.

Garton, A.F. and Pratt, C. (1989). *Learning to be Literate: The Development of Spoken and Written Language*. 2nd edn. Oxford: Blackwell Press.

Gee, J. (1996). *Social Linguistics and Literacies: Ideology in Discourse*. London: Falmer Press.

Vygotsky, L. (1986). *Thought and Language*. Cambridge, MA: MIT Press.

White, R. (1988). *Learning Science*. Oxford: Blackwell Press.

3

What is it about homework?

Deborah Tranter

What grade did you get for the project?
I got an 'A', which was better than last time.
Oh! I only got a B+.

Surprisingly, this was not two students talking, but their parents. It was part of a conversation overheard at a local football training session. The conversation was between the parents of two Grade 5 students. They were discussing their children's homework.

INTRODUCTION

In my experience as a teacher, conversations like the one quoted above are not unusual. Reflecting on conversations of this nature has, over the years, led me to question the purpose and value of homework as a means of improving children's learning. How equitable is homework when teachers have: little influence over the home learning environment; lack an understanding of the home conditions affecting many children; and know little of the quality of assistance that their students will receive? Should we even consider questions of equality when we live in a highly competitive society? Arguably, the well-educated and financially secure families have huge advantages in terms of access to resources, knowledge, private tutors and other assistance. Conversely, for some children, completing any schoolwork at home may not be possible, as they may be concerned with basic issues that most of us take for granted, such as personal safety, adequate sleep and food.

BACKGROUND TO THE STUDY

When I began my career as a teacher in an English secondary school, I soon became aware of the problems associated with children having an unsupportive home environment for their learning. One day, one of my Year 7 students told me:

> I can't take school books home. My Dad just rips them up and throws them on the fire.

My interest in homework as a research topic began four years ago when I was teaching a Grade 4 class. One of my students, whenever he was asked how he was getting along with his homework project, replied using the pronoun 'we'. For example, 'We have done the drawings' or 'We have started the writing'. On the due date, he came into the classroom with a superbly written and illustrated piece of work, immediately followed by his eager mother who asked: 'When are you displaying the projects?'

I asked her a number of questions, and her answers confirmed my suspicions that she had actually done *all* the project work herself. However, she was prepared to justify her input by stating that her son John had 'traced over the words and read a page of the encyclopedia'.

John had some learning difficulties and was not a good reader, but his mother had very high expectations of him. After further discussion, it appeared to me that John's mother's motive for doing his homework was linked to her own status in relation to other parents.

Later that term, another one of my students handed in his homework. It was in his mother's handwriting. When I asked her why she wanted homework set for her son, she replied that 'homework gives parents an insight into what their child is learning at school and, more importantly, how they are coping with that work'. It took me a long time to convince this parent that it was acceptable for her son to hand in work that was not *all* correct. I explained that it was *his* work that I needed to see so that I had an indication of where *he* needed assistance. It became apparent that she knew her son needed help but that she did not want other parents to notice—status again was important.

The prevailing public attitude of the wealthier Western nations towards homework has, over the last century, cycled from positive to negative, and back again (Cooper et al., 1998). At the beginning of the twentieth century, the memorisation of facts and information was an important learning strategy and, as this could easily be achieved at home, homework was seen as a high priority. In the 1940s, when problem-solving abilities and student interest and initiative were seen to underpin learning, homework was viewed as a punishment and as an intrusion on private home-based activities. This trend was reversed ten years later in the 1950s when knowledge acquisition again became important and then, in the mid-1960s, public opinion turned back away from homework, as it came to be seen as detrimental to students' health and a symptom of too much pressure to succeed. Today, homework is again seen as an important and necessary part of schooling.

Corno (1996) highlights five widespread, unsupported—but popular—misconceptions relating to homework:

- The best teachers give homework.
- More homework is better than less.
- Parents want their children to have homework.
- Homework supports what children learn in school.
- Homework fosters discipline and personal responsibility.

As part of my initial study into parents' and children's perceptions of homework, I had questioned my class as a whole and recorded their responses. I felt, at this point, that I had some interesting information indicating that children had a clear idea as to the reasons for, and value of, homework but I also felt as though I was only dabbling in a field that, while it offered enormous potential for inquiry, was very complicated (Corno, 1996).

Searching for research papers about homework consumed many weekends, as formal published results seemed relatively few and far between. It was clear to me that if I wanted to draw significant conclusions from my work, the importance of a research method and a structured approach to the collection of data was crucial. I felt that I needed to extend my research to include a larger group of children and parents. Therefore, with the support of other teachers, I presented my survey to all the children in Grades 3 to 6 at my school and collated the results.

RESEARCH QUESTIONS

I have come to see homework as a very complex and contentious issue. Questions about the purpose and value of homework generally elicit a wide range of opinions. The subject tends to raise questions related more to the home environment, resources and ability to access information and the range of students' abilities than to the homework *per se*. I embarked on a research project to explore:

- the attitudes of students, parents and teachers to homework—in terms of its value in promoting learning; and,
- whether these attitudes were supported by research evidence.

In researching these questions, I also examined the type of homework tasks set, the support in terms of assistance at home with homework and the perceived importance of homework.

As a teacher interested in improving my practice, I asked the students for their opinions on the homework tasks they had experienced and their suggestions for tasks that they would find interesting and worthwhile in relation to learning. Their suggestions were incorporated into the grade's homework assignments.

RESEARCH METHOD

Data collection involved conducting individual interviews and discussions with teachers at staff and weekly planning meetings and with parents individually and at School Council Education Committee meetings. In addition, I also distributed formal written surveys to the twelve class teachers and 200 families (parents) at my school. (See appendixes 3.1 and 3.2.)

I later collected data on the students' attitudes to homework. I individually interviewed small groups of students, conducted class discussions with my own grade, and presented a written survey, which was completed in class time, to all the students in Grades 3 to 6 (183 students).

TEACHERS' AND PARENTS' ATTITUDES TOWARDS HOMEWORK

From my interviews, discussions and surveys of teachers and parents, the main purposes of homework were articulated as follows:

- to assist learning;
- as revision, consolidation and reinforcement of class work;
- to communicate what is being taught at school;
- to provide parents with an opportunity to work with their child;
- to prepare students for further study/secondary college;
- to complete work that there is not time for in school;
- to develop study habits/routines, and time management/ organisational skills; and,
- to develop students' responsibility for their own learning.

Our parent information evenings, held at the beginning of every school year to explain our work and educational aims, generally include a significant number of questions from parents relating to homework. Many parents have articulated in these forums—quite strongly—their support for substantial homework, especially in the middle and upper grades. Teachers' comments indicate how these parental attitudes affect not only the teachers' behaviour, but school policies.

> If a school is in competition with a private school then they have to set homework. It is a reality, a fact of life, because of parent perceptions and judgements on the quality of education. They relate it to homework and the quantity of homework. Teachers just play the game.
>
> *Secondary school teacher*

> There is an expectation from parents that there is homework, but it is clearly discriminatory. Homework favours those children whose parents are willing/able to provide the necessary help.
>
> *Teacher (Grade 6)*

> I would rather not set homework as it is a lot of work for the teacher and some children never do it, but parents expect it. A few years ago our school policy was none, or very little homework. We would not get away with that now.
>
> *Teacher (Grade 3/4)*

If these are some of the attitudes influencing teachers when they set homework tasks, how much effort do they put into devising interesting, useful or valuable tasks in terms of the aims outlined above? Parents promoting homework may be motivated by their interest in maximising the educational opportunities for their children in a competitive society, but in so doing they may not be able to discern 'busy work' from a genuine learning activity.

The renewed emphasis on homework was a concern for some of the teachers I surveyed, as they noted that several children in their grades never, or rarely, completed homework.

> Why is it that I never get homework in from the kids who really need to do it, only from the ones who don't need it?
>
> *Teacher (Grade 3/4)*

This response raises several important issues. For example, what is the value of common homework tasks set for students with a wide range of abilities, interests and home backgrounds, and why is homework being set for children who do not appear to require it?

If it is true that children who need to do, or practise, extra work are the main ones not completing homework, then there may well be other factors in those children's lives which influence their learning. More homework may not be the answer!

Clearly, the reasons why some students consistently fail to complete homework are complex. Some students are simply not interested, it's not 'cool', some find it too difficult, others may lack an appropriately supportive learning environment at home.

> Homework is boring. I never do it.
>
> *Grade 5 student*

> Homework? I'm a 10-year-old boy! 10-year-old boys never do homework.
>
> *Grade 5 student*

Interestingly, much of the research on homework—mine included—relies on voluntary participation by families and students. It may be that the parents who support homework are those most likely to reply to such a survey. A large American study, which included a review of 120 studies on homework, stated that:

> this study, along with many conducted before it, relied on the voluntary participation of parents. Voluntary response rates are low, suggesting that parents who do respond are more likely to be positively involved in their children's education. Responding parents are also more likely to be white and less likely to represent low-income families (Cooper et al., 1998, p. 82).

My own survey of parental attitudes elicited responses from less than half of our school's families. Of the 90 families (parents) who replied to the survey, 93 per cent thought that children should have homework. Those who did not support homework cited the following reasons—at similar rates of frequency:

- Children should learn other things at home (life skills).
- They do enough work at school.
- Children should be free to play at home.
- Homework is not necessary at primary (elementary) school.
- Homework could cause children to develop a negative attitude to schoolwork.
- Homework causes problems and disruptions at home especially if the child does not want to do it.

Harris Cooper, an educational psychologist who has reviewed and completed extensive reseach on homework in America, reported (in 1994) that homework often causes considerable friction between children, parents and teachers. In addition, many pediatricians and family doctors indicated that when children reported medical problems, issues with homework were also a frequent cause of concern. The perception by some parents that homework can contribute to the development of a negative attitude in children towards school is also supported in specific cases by research which found that lengthy homework assignments could lead to fatigue, and the extinction of interest in the relevant topic (Cooper et al., 1998). On this basis, it can be argued that, for some children, homework is at best a pointless exercise, at worst, counterproductive.

The majority of parents who participated in my survey stated that homework should begin in the infant grades and concurred with the reasons given by teachers as to its importance.

A minority of parents wanted teachers to assign homework in order to keep their children away from the television, as indicated by these responses from two families of Grade 4 children:

They [children] should have 30 minutes [homework] every night of the week so they don't watch TV.

Give them something challenging every night so as to keep them away from TV when they get home.

Naturally, the teachers at our school were not impressed by this type of response and some were resentful of these parents' 'unrealistic' expectations of the school.

Only 8 per cent of the parents who responded to my survey did not help their children with homework. Sixty-three per cent of parents helped with their children's homework when needed or occasionally and 21 per cent gave help on a regular basis. This is interesting when compared with children's perceptions that 77 per cent of the help given by parents occurs only when needed.

Most parents thought that children should spend from one to three hours per week on homework which should consist of reading, basic literacy and mathematical skills, revision of class work and research projects. These are also the tasks most often assigned as homework.

In one family's response to my parent survey, opposing attitudes to homework were articulated from each parent of one child. The mother fully supported regular academic homework tasks that consisted of reading, mathematics and spelling revision exercises. The father, conversely, was opposed to homework and thought children should be exploring their environment and learning about 'life skills' at home. It had not occurred to me to survey parents separately.

It is interesting to ponder the diversity in teachers' approaches to, and the type and quantity of, homework tasks they set for children. Some teachers also impose lengthy lunchtime detentions on child-ren who fail to complete work, whilst others do not impose any consequences. It therefore seems to me that a teacher's attitude and expectations towards homework, and the type of tasks set, could influence children's attitudes and feelings considerably. In fact, it has been found in American studies that 'more positive teacher attitudes towards homework were associated with more assigned homework' (Cooper et al., 1998, p. 81).

More, or lengthy, homework assignments may also cause lower completion rates and then lower achievement levels for students. Cooper et al. (1998) reviewed nearly 120 studies of homework and also completed research on attitudes to homework and student academic achievement. The conclusions are summarised as follows:

- Homework for older students (mainly secondary school) plays an important role in improving their grades and achievement scores.
- Homework for younger, elementary school students (primary school) has very little effect on achievement gains (however, it may

have long-term benefits in developing study/time management skills which impact on academic achievement in later years).

- Very lengthy homework assignments, for some children, can lead to fatigue and/or unfavourable attitudes towards homework, and can have a negative impact on the interest level of the child in the topic studied.

- Parents' attitudes about homework have direct, positive effects on their children's attitudes which, at upper grades, impact on their children's academic achievements. Therefore, efforts to improve parent attitudes to homework are likely to pay off in terms of improved learning.

- Clear communication of homework goals and involvement of parents in the homework process can improve parents' attitudes towards homework.

- Positive teacher attitudes towards homework may affect children's achievements negatively, but indirectly, as longer homework assignments may be set which cause lower completion rates, in turn resulting in poorer grades.

However, this research only investigated the relationship between attitudes and the effectiveness of homework as expressed by academic outcomes. There is a need to broaden the criteria in gauging the effectiveness of homework to include the development of cognitive strategies, study habits and improved motivation. Homework, it appears, does improve academic performance in older students, at least for those families willing to participate in the research projects. As Cooper et al. (1998) conclude, though: 'Further investigators need to find ways to involve families that are typically under represented in homework studies.' (Cooper et al., 1998, p. 81).

STUDENT SURVEY RESULTS: STUDENTS' ATTITUDES TO HOMEWORK

Of the 183 students who completed the survey, 60 per cent liked homework or felt that it was OK and 40 per cent did not like, or hated, homework. Interestingly, when the results were differentiated into middle school (Grades 3/4) and upper school (Grades 5/6) responses, there was a marked difference in attitudes, with 75 per cent of the younger students having a positive attitude to homework, compared with only 44 per cent of the older children.

Of those students in Grades 5/6 who said they did not like homework, and who provided a reason, 50 per cent said it was boring and 50 per cent said it was either 'a waste of time' or that it 'takes up too much of their time'. Importantly, 15 per cent of those who had a positive attitude to homework also added that it 'took up too much of their time'.

There are children who see benefits in homework, despite believing it to be a waste of time, and there also some children who do not like homework, but who still think that they should have it! A significant issue with children appears to be that homework impacts on their out-of-school free time and that they do enough work whilst they are at school. Discussing this with children further uncovers resentment of the 'hijacking' of their free time:

> They (children) get a lot of work at school and they should have some time to themselves.

> We do work at school. We should be able to play with our friends.

> Homework takes away our home time.

> Because home is for fun and 'us' time.
>
> *Grade 5 and 6 students*

The majority of children, like their parents, appear to prefer the types of homework tasks that are actually most often assigned by teachers. These include projects, and Maths and English tasks. However, though more children preferred research projects to Maths tasks, when asked which homework was the most useful, most respondents identified Maths over projects.

The most common homework that is set for children at our school involves project research, Maths and English tasks (number facts, spelling, grammar, etc.). The children's responses must be viewed in the context of their own experiences of homework. I found that, in my Grade 4 class, when I first began to look at designing more interesting homework tasks (and providing a wide variety of homework tasks, such as construction, cooking and Science experiments), I received a much greater variety of suggestions and ideas from the children as to their preferred type of homework. The children's opinions may therefore be more a reflection of the school's approach to homework than of homework as an intrinsically valuable exercise. Of the children who stated that they should have homework, the majority preferred it only once per week, beginning from Grades 1 to 4.

On reflection, I should have confidentially noted the names of the children on each survey form in order to ascertain possible correlations between attitude and gender or ability. I certainly noticed that many, but not all, of the very negative written responses also were completed in poor handwriting and with many spelling mistakes. This would be interesting to follow up as, originally, I had encouraged anonymity in order to promote honest responses. However, I have found that children are very keen to express their opinions if they believe something positive may result. They tend to trust the teacher and often only require assurances that they are not going to get into trouble for being honest!

On collating the survey responses, I did find it sad to read statements from children as young as nine or ten who explained that homework made them feel:

Dumb.

Like someone who can't do it.

Terrible.

Nervous, terrified, dumb.

These were a minority of children, but I suspected that they included those who needed a great deal of extra help with their work. Homework appeared to be just another area of failure for them, probably reinforcing their low self-esteem. It would seem that children do not all benefit equally from homework. Notwithstanding these types of comments, many children did find homework assignments to be 'great' or 'fun'. This could be related to home or teacher attitudes, ability or type of homework tasks given.

MY INTERVENTION

As part of my initial study into parents' and children's perceptions of homework, I had questioned my grade as a whole and recorded their responses.

Grade 4 students' perceptions of homework

Negative points

- Some is too hard—don't understand it—the whole family has to help.
- Too easy/too hard.
- It is boring.
- Don't like working at home—we do enough at school.
- We miss out on the TV/computer.
- Takes up our play/free time.
- Don't have time.

Positive points

- It helps us to learn.
- Mums and Dads get to help.
- We don't forget things we learn at school.
- It keeps us busy.
- We can't copy people.

I then asked the grade about the reasons they thought they were given homework and wrote their replies on the board.

Why do you think teachers give out homework?

- To make your brain think after school.
- So that we can learn.
- Parents like homework.
- So we aren't just working at school.
- I don't know—it helps us learn but I don't know how.
- Because it's a school and that is what schools get paid for. I'm here to learn.
- Homework does help you to learn but I never do it anyway. Homework is boring.

Why do you think parents like homework?

- We don't get everything done at school.
- Parents like to see our work and see what we are doing at school.
- So that parents can have a rest (while their children work).
- To practise for secondary school.
- To help us remember the answers (Maths).
- To help us to learn.
- So we are working at home, not playing all the time.
- We learn different things than at school.
- So we don't do it all in one day.

Additionally, I surveyed and interviewed the children in my grade (Grade 4) on their perceptions, attitudes and the types of homework that they preferred. My aim was to develop homework tasks that were relevant to their interests and abilities as well as to inspire and motivate learning. However, though I was not prepared to cancel homework altogether—partly due to perceived parental pressure—I did allow for some 'homework-free' weeks on request from the children. As a class, we negotiated the term's homework, based on the current unit of work and the children's interests. The children were given a choice of tasks and activities. This was a successful exercise, as evidenced by very positive feedback from a large majority of parents and students and an increase in the homework completion rate (up to 100 per cent for many children). I found the children's perceptions very interesting. For example, many of the homework tasks suggested by the children involved their special interests. This could mean making models and finding out information, writing stories or researching their football team. Suggestions included:

- Making a model of an animal and finding out a little about it.
- Making a model of a tadpole changing into a frog.
- Building a model ship and explaining how it works.
- Picking a football player and finding out his history.
- Writing a mythical story about dragons, witches and wizards.
- Inventing an insect and writing about it.
- Designing a Tamagotchi and writing about how it works.
- Drawing your favourite football team, colouring it and writing some of the player's names.
- Building an animal house and writing about how you made it.
- Getting a caterpillar and seeing how it grows.
- Sewing.

I later extended my homework investigations to the other grades in my area of the middle primary school. The success rate in terms of all homework being completed, and satisfaction expressed by parents and children, was excellent when we set a choice of homework tasks that catered for a variety of interests, abilities and learning styles. For example, we used tasks based on Bloom's (1956) Taxonomy and Gardiner's (1983) Multiple Intelligences from which children selected two or three preferred activities to be completed over a period of two weeks. The completed work was then displayed in the class, or was presented to the other children in the case of musical, oral or theatrical tasks. This provided immediate feedback and recognition of the work completed.

To cater for a few children whose home situations appeared less supportive, as stated by the children or from my own observations of non-completion of previous homework assignments, I provided some time in class as catch-up or homework sessions. I also provided construction materials for the homework to assist those children who may not have been able to access such materials at home.

When presenting their finished tasks to the grade, parental help was acknowledged. From my discussions, I ascertained that many children felt that homework should be completed without much help from others. Those children who presented fantastic models that obviously demonstrated significant adult input were questioned in detail by the others as to exactly what their own contribution had been. Model-making, especially those where cutting and power tools were needed, provided some valuable insights. Several children (boys and girls) stated that their fathers had enjoyed being involved—usually it was the children's mothers who checked or helped with homework. The issue of gender-based parental support in homework is a largely unexplored area. The extent to which children can access the support of both parents may be of some significance. Similarly, the attitudes of fathers and mothers may vary and, in a society with a significant number of single-parent families, this is an issue worthy of further study.

CONCLUSION

Most of the parents and students I surveyed and interviewed had strong opinions about homework and its value to learning. Their opinions seemed to be grounded in tradition and perception rather than specific personal experiences. The majority of parents were in favour of a substantial amount of homework (up to three hours per week at primary school), consisting of consolidation in basic skills in Maths and English. They provided help mainly in explaining the work to their children and articulated the purposes of homework as assisting in improving learning, developing time management and study skills, preparation for the future (e.g. secondary school) and communicating the school's programs to parents.

It is my concern that homework, given the wide diversity of atti-tudes and resources available in the home, is not an equitable exercise for children in that it can promote disadvantage or advantage, depend-ing on family circumstances. If education is concerned with providing a 'level playing field' of opportunity for children, how does home-work contribute equally to the education of all children? Which families benefit most from homework, in terms of broad educational achievement, and to what extent does homework currently reinforce, rather than redress, the link between academic achievement and socio-economic background?

I believe that the topic of homework provides a wide range of research possibilities. These include studies on families generally under-represented in homework studies to date, and the relationship, if any, between attitude and success in homework and socio-economic status. I have found few research findings linking student attitudes, and the volume of homework completed, to improved study habits.

PERSONAL REFLECTION

In terms of personal growth, one of the most important things that I have learnt is that, in trying to find the answers to what I initially believed were fairly basic questions—for example, 'What is a valuable homework task?'—I have mainly succeeded in raising a great many more questions.

Throughout my teaching career, I have always been interested in the value of academic research; however, from my observations, this is not a view widely shared by many of my colleagues in primary schools. Teachers are busy practitioners with an increasing workload related to new teaching directions and welfare issues. I have, however, found that, without overloading oneself, some reflective classroom research can be a means of broadening horizons and inspiring one's own learning. This learning becomes much more valuable if it can then be shared with others and used to improve teaching practice.

What started initially as a broad and general topic on the value of homework in relation to learning generally became more focused on issues of equity as I progressed through my study. With hindsight, my study should have been refined to small areas that were easier to research. In fact, my main findings have been to highlight gaps in the homework research generally, thus creating more questions than answers for me.

On reflection, as a teacher-researcher, I may be—initially—just like my younger students who, when asked to complete a project, choose a topic such as 'The Sea' or 'Space'. The role of the teacher then is to narrow down the study to a practical and manageable size. Similarly, I chose a wide-ranging topic and set out to follow up a few interesting leads—not always in an organised and systematic fashion. Discussion of my ideas, plans and findings with researchers who are experienced in this area has been of great benefit. In retrospect, as a full-time teacher and leader at my school, I did not have enough time to fully plan and implement my research method and this is something I would like to better develop in the future.

This year, as an assistant principal in a new school, I do not teach in the classroom nor assign homework personally. However, my leadership position enables me to influence other teachers directly and via the school's policies. In encouraging my colleagues to reflect on the quality, and quantity, of homework tasks set in our school, I share my ideas and model a range of assignments that I have found to be relevant to students' learning, successful and enjoyable for both parents and children. I actively promote a teaching style and, where homework is set, home tasks that cater for a range of students' talents and abilities within each grade, in addition to those which are interesting, practical and linked to the curriculum. By articulating my research findings, promoting educational discussion and raising questions, I hope to raise school and community awareness of the problematic nature of homework tasks.

REFERENCES

Bloom, B. (ed.) (1956). *Taxonomy of Educational Objectives: The Classification of Educational Goals*. Handbook I. Cognitive Domain. New York: David McKay.

Corno, L. (1996). Homework is a Complicated Thing. *Educational Researcher,* 25 (8), 27–30.

Cooper, H. (1991). Homework. *Feelings and the Medical Significance,* 33 (2), 7–10.

—— (1994). *The Battle over Homework. An Administrator's Guide to Setting Sound and Effective Policies*. The Practicing Administrator's Leadership Series. Thousand Oaks, CA: Corwin Press.

Cooper, H., Lindsay, J.J., Nye B. and Greathouse, S. (1998).

Relationships Among Attitudes About Homework, Amount of Homework Assigned and Completed, and Student Achievement. *Journal of Educational Psychology*, 90 (1), 70–83.

Gardner, H. (1983) *Frames of Mind: The Theory of Multiple Intelligences*. New York: Basic Books.

APPENDIX 3.1: PARENT SURVEY

Name (optional)   *Child's Grade level*

1. Do you think children should have homework? Why/why not?
2. What do you think is the importance of homework?
3. At which grade level do you think homework should start?
4. How much help do you give your child/children with homework?
5. What type of help do you provide?
6. How much time per week do you think should be spent on homework?
7. What kind of homework do you think is the most useful?
8. Any other comments.

APPENDIX 3.2: TEACHER SURVEY

Name (optional)   *Grade level*

1. Do you think that students in your grade should have homework?
2. If so, why?
3. At what levels of schooling do you think homework is valuable and why?
4. What kind and quantity of homework do you set for your grade (and how often)?
5. What sort of feedback do you receive from parents regarding homework?
6. Do some students have problems with homework, or with handing it in on time, etc. in your grade? If so, what and how do you deal with these problems?

7. Do you set different homework tasks for students with different interests or abilities? (Why or why not?)
8. How much input/help from parents regarding their child's homework do you expect?
9. Do you have any problems regarding too much or not enough help or support from parents regarding their child's homework?
10. Any other comments.

APPENDIX 3.3: STUDENT HOMEWORK SURVEY

Grade level

1. How do you feel about homework?
2. Do you think children should have homework? Why?
3. What homework do you think is the most useful?
4. What homework do you like best?
5. If you could choose anything for homework what would you choose? Why?
6. How much do your parents help you with homework?
7. How much time each week should children have homework?
8. At what grade level should homework start?
9. Any other comments.

'I don't want to be here': Engaging reluctant students in learning

Meaghan Walsh with Marilyn Smith

INTRODUCTION

This chapter outlines the experiences associated with supporting an action research project that was conducted during 1999 by Marilyn Smith, a Year 11 English teacher at Corio Community College. Corio is a senior secondary college (Years 11 and 12 only) in Geelong (Victoria's second largest city) and draws on a mainly low socio-economic population.

Marilyn aimed to adapt the Year 11 English Syllabus to the needs of a group of 20 male students, characterised as 'non-academic'. She hoped that tailoring the subject material and tasks to this particular group of students would help engage them in English, and ultimately assist them in succeeding in this compulsory school subject.

The main data collection was conducted by Meaghan through interviews with a sample of students from the class. The initial interviews were conducted early in the school year to obtain baseline information about the students' attitudes towards school, learning and English. A follow-up interview was carried out towards the end of the year, to identify any significant shifts in the students' views and experience after the 'changed' teaching period.

RATIONALE FOR THE RESEARCH PROJECT: BACKGROUND INFORMATION

Marilyn's first year at the school shocked her. The Year 11 boys just kept leaving school. She had not experienced this before and was astonished to find such a high degree of 'disengagement' from students. She was likewise surprised at the apparent acceptance of this exodus by the staff. For example, when Marilyn queried the large number of students in her class at the beginning of the year, she received amused assurances from staff that 'They won't be here for long'.

Marilyn describes how she saw the students and the school situation they were in:

> The whole idea of school and academic learning was entirely alien and irrelevant to both their experience and their life goals. Successful men did not read books, had little use for written language in any form and did not take instruction from women, especially bloody know-all English teachers.
>
> School was demoralising, and had no system of rewards that had any congruence with their values. For these boys (and lots of other 'boys' out there) it was 'cool to be a fool'—getting a good mark for English or being praised by a teacher, especially a middle-aged female middle-class English teacher, had all the appeal of being kissed by a moustached aunt!
>
> If they could have any sort of job they would not be at school—the only reason to attend—as little as possible—was to get the piece of paper.
>
> The curriculum was indisputably out of date and completely inappropriate for these students.
>
> The texts and the syllabus would have been entirely appropriate for an academic high school in the eastern suburbs in the 1960s (which is where most of the teachers either went to school or received their training). The recent addition of

Sally Morgan's *My Place* was no doubt introduced with all the good intentions of anti-racist feminists, but was actually used as an instrument of oppression in precisely the way that gave political correctness a bad name. It actually made being racist the only option for these boys.

The prevailing teaching styles were passive, rote, author-itarian, punitive and focused on inevitable failure. The teachers were 'doing their best' but the 'kids here' were 'just not up to it'. Emphasis on welfare avoided scrutiny of the impoverished curriculum and hostile classroom environment. The kids had nowhere else to go but they sure didn't want to be here.

Few classrooms were interactive, experiential or rewarding and the poor literacy understandings of the staff were per-petuated in the students. There was a sense that someone, somewhere else, was to blame.

This is my memory of the school in my first year there. It was very different from the school I had come from about 4 kilometres away. Since then there have been some marked improvements, not the least was the setting up of a PEEL group with the appointment of the new Assistant Principal, Steve Boyle.

In that first year at the school, Marilyn found herself policing interminable chapter summaries of Sally Morgan's *My Place* and discovering that many boys made the decision (which seemed completely rational to them) that they would rather fail their VCE (Victorian Certificate of Education: the final two years of secondary schooling) than continue on to Chapter 24. When she discussed this problem at the faculty level, suggesting that this book was not an appropriate text for these boys, she was admonished with a response that 'if the boys couldn't cope with this sort of book then they don't "deserve" to get their VCE'.

From her point of view, this appeared to be sacrificing one group of students without doing anything to assist them with the task of achieving some level of competency in their literacy skills. Marilyn tried to find out something about their past experiences that might explain the attitudes they now held:

The students had been identified as unlikely to pass VCE, they had poorly developed English skills, and in all cases almost no confidence in their abilities. I asked them to write a case study each about something that had turned them off English in the past. All of them had had particularly miserable experiences in English classes particularly at the lower levels—experiences which included being publicly humiliated for their poor skills. They had all been frequently punished, usually for their refusal to carry out particular tasks that they found demeaning or excessive, their boisterous behaviour, or their socially unskilled behaviour. It seemed they been punished for the very things they had not learned or been taught.

For Marilyn, this was a starting point for a teaching approach, and subsequent project, that might address these concerns. The school had undergone a shift in philosophy, which established a more flexible approach toward catering for the needs of 'non-academic' students, and initiated strategies that would support wider definitions of success at the senior levels. This context, combined with an increasing confidence in the theories and strategies generated by PEEL and her involvement with Innovative Links and 'Boys' Education', convinced Marilyn that there was no reason why boys could not be assisted in succeeding in English at the VCE level.

She believed that it was possible to engage these students in learning English, and that raising their awareness of their learning styles and processes would assist this. By enabling the students to see and understand the barriers to their school success, she considered that she might be able to unlock their capacity to take what they needed from the curriculum for their own sense of literacy success and use.

AIMS OF THE RESEARCH

Marilyn's ultimate goal was to assist her 20 male students to succeed in the compulsory subject of English, and to improve their use of English in subjects such as Technology and Wood/Metalwork, which more closely represented their career aspirations and source of self-worth.

She began by establishing a 'boys only' group for Year 11 English, which would concentrate on completing one unit only for the year, rather than the prescribed two units (to gain their VCE, students in Victoria [Australia] need to pass three out of four units of English including Units 3 and 4). Marilyn realised that these students would probably experience greater success at this level if the curriculum was responsive to their interests and preoccupations.

> I felt the problem was more to do with the curriculum than the students' apparent inability to learn English to a reasonable standard. Many people believe that the VCE curriculum is too academic, but also we have tended not to exploit its possibilities—we have a fixation with testing that the kids have read every page and completed endless comprehension tasks. The whole issue of assessment means that they don't have time to comfortably learn. My intention was get away from this and exploit the flexibility to see if we could get them to the point where they had met the work requirements of Unit 1.

HOW DID PAVOT CONTRIBUTE TO THE PROJECT?

Marilyn's concerns for her students and her workload made it very difficult for her to both address her concerns and research them simultaneously. PAVOT funds allowed me [Meaghan] to become Marilyn's research associate. I worked with Marilyn in the initial process of defining and operationalising the research aims and methodology. We decided that I would conduct the data collection in the form of one-to-one interviews with students, then qualitatively analyse the data for significant themes and issues and report the information to Marilyn to inform her practice.

THE RESEARCH PROCESS: WHAT DID WE DO?

Marilyn wanted some essential preliminary information about her students:

1. their current attitude towards school, their learning and perceived barriers to effective learning, their career aspirations, and specifically their attitude towards English; and
2. their awareness of good learning, and the effectiveness of their strategies for planning tasks, organising their workload to meet deadlines and revision.

She also wanted to identify any shifts in the students' attitude following her attempts to address these concerns in her teaching.

Over several meetings, Marilyn and I established that the research plan would involve:

- preliminary interviews with students;
- feedback of this data to Marilyn;
- a nine-month teaching intervention; and,
- follow-up student interviews.

Preliminary interview with students

Confidential one-to-one interviews were conducted with a sample of ten students from the class (50 per cent) who had volunteered for the task. These interviews were designed to explore these students' views on several aspects of their learning and future career plans including:

- perception of self as a learner (with particular focus on English);
- perception of English;
- level of awareness of the learning process (i.e. what it means to be a 'good learner');
- level of organisation (i.e. skills for completing assessment tasks/revision strategies);
- perceived social barriers to academic success (with particular focus on English);
- awareness of 'school' as an option in the context of alternative choices available; and,
- intended future direction: the role that school was expected to play in the student's career path.

With the students' permission, the interviews were audio-taped and a content analysis was conducted on the transcriptions to identify significant themes or issues raised by the sample.

Perception of self as a learner (with particular focus on English)
The students characterised themselves as generally being 'reasonably good' students. They did, however, tend to hold less esteem for themselves as English students. They explained this difference in terms of a difficulty in grasping the concepts in English, and also the skills that they were supposed to be developing in the subject. Only one student indicated that he had a good understanding of the material and tasks in English.

Perception of English
The majority of students felt that there was no aspect of English that they found enjoyable. Tasks associated with writing were considered by most students to be the least enjoyable aspect of English.

Level of awareness of the learning process (i.e. what it means to be a 'good learner')
The students generally believed that they had a solid conceptual grasp in a least one of their subjects; however, English was only referred to once in this manner. The practical or technical subjects were the areas where students felt they had a greater understanding of the main ideas, because the practical exercises offered an opportunity to apply and contextualise the theory. That is, the connection between topic and task was quite apparent to them. The general view was that the nature of English often made it difficult to identify how the task was meant to link in with the current topic:

> Sometimes it's hard in English, it's not clear cut like practical subjects.

Interestingly, a 'good learner' was typically characterised as someone in possession of one or more innate and static qualities that were perceived to be outside a student's control, such as:

They are just brainy.

Brighter than everyone.

They naturally understand what the teacher is saying.

Very few students referred to characteristics of a good student's work ethic or aspects of good organisation or purposeful learning. Those who did refer to such factors still believed that success only came if you were lucky enough to possess a combination of the 'good wiring' and a commitment to completing the necessary work.

Level of organisation (i.e. skills for completing assessment tasks/revision strategies)

In terms of planning for assignments and other assessment tasks, only a small minority of students applied a proactive approach to completing their work, with the majority indicating that they employed the 'last-minute' approach. None of the students could expand upon their method for completing such tasks beyond 'I just do it'.

The group also employed some fairly passive revision strategies for tests, with the majority indicating that they simply had a quick look over their notes the night before the test. Only one person engaged in active revision by doing some exercises in preparation for Maths tests.

Perceived social barriers to academic success (particular focus on English)

The majority of the students could not identify any external pressure from family or friends to leave school and work, with most indicating that their family was supportive of their progression to Year 11 and were encouraging them to continue with their study.

They did, however, describe a significant cultural barrier to academic success within their peer group at school. There was a clear social perception that a 'good student' was:

Nerdy.

Has no friends.

Just has school and that's it.

Sucks up to the teachers.

The students clearly indicated that this was not good for their image. They could not be seen as good learners or good students by their peers. One person actually said that he lied about his marks to avoid the 'good student' tag:

> You just keep it to yourself when you get a good mark, tell people you got a C when you got an A, you have to fit in.

Awareness of 'school' as an option in the context of alternative choices available
All the students indicated that they had made a conscious decision to return to school and at least commence the VCE, stating that they took the option to continue study as it constituted a necessary step in their career.

Intended future direction: The role that school was expected to play in the students' career path
Every student appeared to have well-defined career goals, outlining a particular career path they intended to follow. They also demonstrated an awareness of the level of education required for their intended career and seemed to have factored the necessary amount of extra schooling into their plan. Half of the students aimed to complete the VCE as they needed passes in Year 12 to access certain apprenticeships or progress to some form of higher education.

Intervention phase: Nine-month teaching period

Marilyn used the feedback from the interview data to plan her teaching intervention. The three main components involved:

1. designing activities and selecting texts that she believed would be both challenging to the students and accessible in terms of their skill level;
2. negotiating a 'deal' with the class that if she could not convince the students that a particular activity had some value for them and their future aspirations, they would discontinue the task; and,
3. employing many PEEL teaching procedures, particularly those based on cultivating questioning (question dice) and encouraging reflection.

Marilyn focused on designing activities and selecting texts that she felt the students would find accessible, in terms of her perception of their skill level, and that would be challenging in both their ideas and their content. The texts she chose included *Tomorrow, When the War Began* (John Marsden), *Wake in Fright* and the film texts *In the Name of the Father* and *The Shawshank Redemption*. One interesting feature which affected student response to a text was whether or not it was a true story. For this reason, they liked *In the Name of the Father* much more than *The Shawshank Redemption*. Marilyn 'allowed them' to believe that *Wake in Fright* was based on a true story for that purpose.

Marilyn negotiated a deal with the class that, if she could not convince them that a particular activity had some value for them and their future aspirations, the group would stop doing the task—clearly a risky and unusual teaching approach.

Her activities were based on:

* football team results;
* local media issues and letters to the editor of the local paper;
* career path research;
* research on topics of particular interests; and,
* the use of computer technology, especially the Internet.

Marilyn describes how they used technology:

We used technology a lot, especially the Internet. I got them to research a career they were interested in. This was hugely successful because they were highly motivated, and I found it quite ironic to watch them in the careers room, studiously reading and sharing books without even realising what they were doing! They had to do a Powerpoint presentation on their career. We hyperlinked them all together and gave a class presentation to an invited audience.

We did a lot of work on media. I had them writing to the *Geelong Advertiser* [their local newspaper] about Gary Ablett's [a famous local Australian Rules footballer, now retired] statue. They loved reading the local newspaper. It was real, it was a local paper and they could identify the issues as theirs.

Marilyn also used many PEEL strategies, especially those based on cultivating questions (question dice) and encouraging reflection (see Baird and Northfield, 1992). Marilyn hoped that, by raising the students' awareness of *how* successful learning took place in English and *why* this might be valuable, she might be able to increase their level of engagement in the material and tasks:

> They needed tasks they could complete and they needed instant feedback. For example, with the novel *Tomorrow, When the War Began*, I didn't make them do the normal written text response. I negotiated with them that if they read the book they could use the question dice. These are a set of two die: one has the words who, what, where, when, how and why on it, and the other has would, could, might, did and should. Students throw the dice and use the resulting stem to begin a question, for example, 'What might . . .?' They found these entertaining and quite difficult—they very rarely got up into 'How might . . .?', for example. However, they worked in groups and got feedback from each other and myself, and I used the opportunity to unpack the idea that asking questions is an important aspect of learning.

She also modified a version of the L Files booklets (see Chapter 9) and, following a suggestion from one of the other PAVOT teachers, set the boys the task of writing case studies about their experiences of learning in primary and junior secondary school. She noted that the L Files 'Fell apart completely. One of the peer leaders said, "No. I don't want to do this." That killed it.'

This incident raises the issue of the major problem Marilyn faced in implementing this program:

> This was supposed to be a small group of carefully chosen boys who would do unit one English for the whole year. It wasn't meant to be a group of the worst boys in the level, it was the boys that you felt you could help. A major problem was that this criterion wasn't adhered to.
>
> One cause was that government policy changed and we had returnees trickling back to school—they had to attend school to get government benefits—the dole (unemployment benefits). Many of these students ended up in the class without necessarily meeting the criteria we'd set. We had kids who were illiterate right through to kids who were competent but who just did not want to be at school.
>
> Having students trickle in completely ruined the dynamic of the class. I had set out to establish trust, but having to frequently incorporate new students made this impossible. A lot of the 'selected' boys were quite threatened by some of the newcomers, some of whom were 19 and 20 years old, and a couple of them were quite frightening characters.
>
> For first term we had to just mark time. The boys were constantly trying to regroup—they would establish the pecking order and then they'd have to change it.
>
> I had running battles with the school administration, but they didn't have many choices either. All of these things are done within such a political context. My group was supposed to be small, for educational reasons; however, that meant that all the other English classes were bigger, and this caused some resentment as well. When new students came in, the 'obvious' place to put them was in the smallest class.

For this reason, in particular, Marilyn was unable to implement her stated aim of developing the boys' awareness of, and control over, their own learning to the extent that she had hoped. The L Files were meant to be the catalyst for leading them into discussions about learning, and ultimately into becoming more independent and purposeful learners. At the end of Term 1, another arrangement was made for the forced returnees and more progress was possible.

Follow-up student interviews

A second round of one-to-one interviews was conducted with ten volunteer students from the class (six from the original interview sample), to reassess their views on the same constructs and therefore ascertain whether there had been any shifts in their attitudes over the teaching intervention period.

The second interview results suggested that the students had made a number of perceptual and attitudinal shifts over the teaching intervention period. Each significant area of change is outlined below.

General rise in confidence and feelings of control regarding English
The vast majority of students interviewed indicated that they had greater feelings of confidence with regard to English. They primarily described an ability to understand the main concepts covered in the curriculum and also the fact that they were completing the assessment tasks and submitting them on time (or even before the deadline in some cases).

Increased enjoyment of English tasks
This time students were able to quickly identify at least one enjoyable aspect of their English subject. They often raised the fact that having some ownership over the decisions made about the tasks they were to complete made the subject, on the whole, more enjoyable. The tasks involving technology, such as developing a Powerpoint presentation around a particular career, were identified as the most enjoyable specific aspect for most of the students. Some of the students also found the class discussions (about a novel's content) to be very enjoyable.

Greater understanding of the purpose of English tasks

All of the students indicated that, in most cases, they understood why they were doing the set tasks in English. That is, they saw some relevance to their future as job seekers, tertiary students and eventually employees.

This response was certainly in accord with Marilyn's own perception of the way her boys were working. She felt that the students began to accept tasks as both relevant and achievable and that they appeared to really enjoy some of the assessment activities.

View of the school as caring and supportive

The students generally characterised the differences between their involvement in this secondary college and their previous school experience in terms of the fact that teaching staff were more respectful of students. Marilyn's classroom experiences similarly supported this response. The students' case studies about their experience of learning in primary and junior secondary school illustrated that these boys had developed feelings of humiliation and unfair treatment in the past that had created a sense of 'lack of respect'.

RESEARCH METHODOLOGY ISSUES: SOME CONSIDERATIONS FOR CONDUCTING RESEARCH OF THIS NATURE IN FUTURE

It was unfortunate, but part of schooling, that only six of the ten original interview participants were available for a follow-up interview nine months later. There were also a number of other interesting methodological issues or challenges associated with supporting a research project of this kind.

The interview process

I found that eliciting thoughtful responses from students in the interviews was challenging. As per my previous experience with interviewing Year 10–11 students, most of the boys were not immediately forthcoming with responses during our discussion. There are a variety of possible reasons for this, including the age of the participants, gender difference (female interviewer), talking to a stranger, and also the fact that it is unlikely that they had ever been directly asked to explore many of the issues that were raised during the interview.

In order to draw out as much information from the participants as possible, I employed several strategies such as prompting and probing, switching to simpler questions about the student's interests, discussion of light topics such as hobbies, using humour, and sharing personal stories about my school experiences. As such, extra time was occasionally required to complete the interview protocol with a student.

Ethical challenge to preserve the participants' identity in reporting the interview outcomes

As the interview sample consisted of ten students who were known to Marilyn, careful consideration was required in planning the interviews in order to preserve their ethical right of confidentiality. In the initial interview, it was decided that no individual would be identified in the reporting of the outcomes, and that any anecdotal material (i.e. pithy quotes to illustrate or encapsulate a particular point) would not contain any information that would personally identify that individual to Marilyn.

This issue was of even greater significance in the follow-up interview phase, when it was decided that Marilyn would take responsibility for the analysis of the interview transcripts to ascertain what kinds of perceptual and experiential shifts had taken place. A compromise was reached in order to preserve the anonymity of the sample, in that I processed the interview transcripts to such a degree that individuals could not be identified in the commentary, but the data were still preserved in a somewhat 'raw' state. Marilyn could then analyse the content for significant themes or issues and identify any shifts, with minimal risk of recognising one of her students.

WHAT ADVICE WOULD MARILYN OFFER TO TEACHERS TRYING TO DO A SIMILAR THING IN THE FUTURE?

There must be some up-front discussion with these students about what the point and value of the subject is for them. I genuinely believe that for many students, the purpose of many English tasks is not obvious and is not rational. They are not just being provocative when they ask 'Why do we have to do this?' and I believe they are entitled to an answer. The value of this ongoing dialogue as a tool for discussing metacognitive and learning processes, and the purposes of learning, is very significant. I believe that this sort of dialogue actually defines the relationship the teacher has with the class; the role that the teacher takes in this discussion demonstrates whether the students can respect and trust the teacher.

Good learning behaviours needs to be an ongoing theme. A system which constantly identifies and rewards good learning seems to me to be really fundamental. The rewards must be rewards that the students recognise, not necessarily the teacher. (In my class this was not handled successfully because in the initial stages of the class there was a constant stream of newcomers, many transient, which was very unsettling. This prevented me from establishing the atmosphere of trust between me and the boys, and among the boys at that crucial setting-the-scene stage. Later on, the introduction of these ideas was not seen as a fundamental of the class.

There has to be room for interactive and active learning. Competitions, movement around the room, group activities, rolling dice, making products—anthologies, Powerpoint presentations—the opportunities to show off and be funny, daring and risqué are all, it seems to me, entirely legitimate learning methods.

Resources such as newspapers, magazines, Internet and factual written material, manuals, biography and some film and television material are much more profitable learning resources than novels or textbooks (although these obviously have a place if well chosen).

Connecting what they are doing in school with their future lives as men, citizens, workers, fathers, husbands, sportsmen, travellers, adventurers, etc. is a fundamental way of engaging them. Activities such as researching a career, writing letters to newspapers about issues that concern them (such as where should Gary Ablett's statue be placed?) are essential.

Above all, we need to acknowledge that the school system has probably let them down at some stage and persuade them that the things they have not been able to successfully learn so far are not irretrievable and probably not their own fault.

OUTCOMES OF THE RESEARCH

To what extent were the project aims achieved?

Marilyn felt that she achieved a number of her goals, primarily in contributing to the students' success in Year 11 English, and therefore keeping them at school with some options for wider success. She also felt that her research project supported the notion that the VCE structure can be adapted to the needs of different student groups, as she was able to significantly engage her students' attention and interest by tailoring tasks to their particular interests and aspirations.

She was, however, ambivalent about the viability of focusing on metacognitive processes in any overt way. She felt that the careful selection of topics, activities and texts was much more important in engaging her students than any attempt to raise their awareness of their own learning. Marilyn also found that the PEEL strategies were invaluable as the underpinning of her efforts to promote active and purposeful learning.

REFERENCES

Baird, J.R. and Northfield, J.R. (1992). *Learning from the PEEL Experience*. Melbourne: Monash University.

Cook, K. (1971). *Wake in Fright*. Harmondsworth: Penguin.

Marsden, J. (1993). *Tomorrow, When the War Began*. Sydney: Pan Macmillan.

5

Disasters and metacognition in the SOSE classroom

Lynn Boyle

INTRODUCTION

I've asked if I can take my Year 7 class through to Year 8 SOSE (Studies of Society and the Environment) next year. Not because they are a fantastic class, but because right now I feel totally frustrated at what I perceive as a lack of 'success' with this group. As is the case with any class, there is a wide range of abilities and, as is common, the weaker boys are dominating and intrusive. It seems to me as though the brightest students seem to be floating along with the current—maybe I'm just being tough on myself.

For a long time, I had not really differentiated between teaching and learning. My early belief was that if students were busy completing the set task and they were enjoying it, then surely they must be learning. For years I got a buzz from the success of student engagement—we were all having fun; the students were not just busy, they were engaged. But I had never really considered that what we teach is totally separate from what students learn. For many years prior to my involvement in PEEL, I was of the belief that content was

all-important, that students needed to accumulate a bundle of knowledge if they were to be successful in life, but it was often a challenge
to present that 'knowledge' in an appealing way. During my first few
years in PEEL, I thrived on the engagement students had in the classroom through the implementation of PEEL procedures. It took me a
long time to realise that it is not content that is important; then I
began to understand that engagement was not the answer I was
looking for either. It was a long and challenging path that led me to
the realisation, and then the understanding, that students need to be
metacognitive if they are to be true learners—to reflect on their
learning and to understand what makes a good learner. I also came to
understand that I could assist students to achieve that through the
implementation of PEEL procedures. My teaching journey is taking
me on a frustrating yet rewarding quest for encouraging metacognition
in the students I teach.

My aim in writing this chapter is to acknowledge that good
learning does not come from what traditionally has been seen as
'good teaching', and that engaging students in a classroom activity
does not necessarily equate with good learning. It is certainly true that
students will learn better if they are engaged in the task, but are
teachers always clear on what is important for students to learn? My
focus is not just on the student as a learner, but on the teacher as
learner, which is made explicit in the effect that my research has had
on my approach to teaching.

THE RESEARCH

The aim of my research was to determine whether what I believed
was good teaching equated with good learning. Were students
adopting good learning behaviours in the classroom, and if not, how
could I assist them to do this?

It seemed to me that the obvious year level for trying to determine the answer to my question was Year 7. These are the students
who begin their first year in high school open-minded, eager,
friendly, and often with a thirst for learning. My aim, I thought, was
simple—to measure the development of good learning behaviours

over a minimum of one semester. In so doing I thought I would be able to determine the development of my students' metacognition. Along with the students, I also kept an individual journal. We called these journals 'thinking books' (Swan and White, 1994). My reason for using thinking books was that I imagined them being used regularly and that the road to metacognition would be revealed in many of these journals as we progressed throughout the year.

The first two weeks of the year involved settling in and the Year 7 camp. In week 3, our 'real' classes were to begin. Eager to start my research, I set the first task for the first lesson as an activity based on the students' view of learning. The class was introduced to the 'think, pair, share' procedure based on the question 'What is a good learner?' Each student was given their journal in which to write their initial view; they then shared their view with their neighbours and were told that they could add or take away anything they wanted from their list. The class was then asked to divide into groups of four or five and each group was given a body-size piece of butcher's paper. They were asked to find a space on the floor and then choose one person to draw around so that they had a body shape. On the body, using words or diagrams, they were to label all the characteristics of a good learner. At the end of 20 minutes, each group was to explain their 'good learner' to the rest of the class. Groups busied themselves with enthusiasm and brightly coloured textas (felt markers).

It was at this point that I learnt my first lesson. The Year 7s were not particularly interested in doing what I wanted them to—an outline of a body and lots of labels or diagrams to represent a good learner. They obviously had a different purpose for the task. They wanted to create fantastic looking pictures with beautiful blue eyes or trendy looking clothes, flowers in the background or a motorbike for the 'body' to rest on! They were intent on creating pictures to impress, to busy themselves with what they viewed as important—good pictures (see Figure 5.1).

I realized what was happening five minutes into the activity, but no matter how much I insisted that what they said about the learner was important rather than the quality of the picture, they continued to add extra features and colour neatly.

Figure 5.1:   Good learner poster at the start of the semester

The discussion that followed was supposed to create clarity for all on the qualities of a good learner. Despite what I initially saw as the first of many minor disasters, the responses were revealing, with the majority of students focusing on behaviours: sits quietly; doesn't speak; a thinker; good hand–eye coordination; listens; gives opinions; cooperates; has ideas; uses manners; understands; is observant; wears [school] uniform.

A rather one-sided discussion followed as I pointed out the good learning behaviours (GLBs—see Baird and Northfield, 1992) that could be valuable from their list of behaviours. However, they were not all that interested in being told!

I persisted. Each lesson students were to record a response to a simple question related to good learning behaviours in their journals—questions such as:

What I did today . . .

What I learnt today . . .

To improve my learning I could . . .

What I found was that the comments students wrote were clearly related to the tasks we completed in class rather than to the thinking and learning which may have occurred:

What I did today was draw a map.

What I learnt today was how to draw a map.

Over the next few weeks, I constantly reinforced any GLBs that were displayed, but this seemed to wash over the class and they could rarely articulate which GLBs they had displayed during a lesson, much less over the week. At the same time, I was being driven crazy by unnecessary questions and requests:

Do I have to do a border?

Do I have to stick this in?

Do I have to have a heading?

So-and-so has my ruler!

I felt as if I was drowning. I was tired of the mindless quibble and decided it was time to give them something to think about—Dirty Tricks (Baird and Northfield, 1992; Mitchell and Mitchell, 1997).

We were studying 'The Earth' and had started the class with a POE (Predict, Observe, Explain) (White and Gunstone, 1992) on a diagram of the Earth's interior. From this we researched and constructed new diagrams. Fantastic pictures! The next lesson we reviewed our research from the previous lesson, then I asked the class to copy notes from the board. I proceeded with:

The earth is like a big ball made up of seven layers. The outside layer is hot and sticky, the next layer is like mud and is hard to walk on. There are a lot of watery oceans inside the earth.

Everyone followed instructions. One student commented about the seven layers but continued to copy. Another asked how it was possible to know that the second layer was hard to walk on! No other comments or questions were made. I asked if anyone had a question.

They didn't! I asked them to take out their diagrams from last lesson and to carefully look at these. Again I asked if there were any questions. Still none. They were not involved in any good learning behaviours—questioning, linking or self-monitoring—in any way at all. They were happy to be given meaningless information and to write it neatly in their books. They believed that they were being good students.

Finally I told them that I had just made it all up and that it was all wrong. Chaos erupted. At last some thinking was happening—they started to question me:

> But we trusted you . . .

> We have to follow instructions . . .

> You told us to copy it . . .

> The teacher's always right!

After I had re-established some form of order in the room, we discussed why I decided to do this to them. At last some movement forward:

> So we think before we write . . .

> We just learnt it so we should have remembered it from yesterday . . .

> So we learn to ask good questions . . . so we don't believe everything we read.

This event led to the first entry in their 'thinking books' which actually related to thinking and learning—with over 60 per cent of students responding to 'today I learnt . . .' with comments relating to the fact that they should think before they write. Thirty-nine per cent related to content—learning about the earth—and one student said: 'I learnt my teacher is a liar.'

After that lesson, the students refused to write anything from the board without reading and questioning first.

Despite this small success, I still felt frustrated at the very slow progress I was making on developing metacognitive learners. It was at a PAVOT meeting that I was introduced to a process that temporarily helped lift the rate at which I could introduce GLBs in a consistent and ongoing way. A PEEL colleague, Gill Pinnis, introduced a small booklet she had titled The L Files (see Chapter 9). In good PEEL fashion, I adapted the procedure to the following:

- Each student is presented with their own L Files booklet—each page has a different Good Learning Behaviour on it.
- In handing these out, I told the students that I was concerned that we were not really becoming good learners so we negotiated a process of achieving 'P plates' (probationary plates, analogous to those displayed on the cars of drivers who are in their first year of holding a driver's licence).
- When a student displayed ten of the behaviours twice, they would be presented with a P plate.
- The student had to present their L Files to me and have the iden-tified GLB signed.

This created great interest and immediately the class was thrown into a frenzy of practising good learning behaviours. At the end of each lesson, five minutes were set aside for students to come and justify their claims for having pages signed—students were planning prior to starting work, asking good questions, linking to other subjects or their own experience.

The students' journal responses now began to relate more often to good learning behaviours; however, a few students were quick to give up on the L Files as they saw others progressing rapidly and they felt left behind. These students were not interested in identifying GLBs at all—as if the purpose in identifying them was to achieve your P plate and nothing else.

I felt as if I was on a roller coaster, then came a breakthrough. The highlight of the semester was what in fact began as yet another disaster.

The following narrative describes a PEEL procedure known as a continuum: a procedure which aims to encourage attention to the task, reflective thinking, retrieval of prior views, linking and the ability to justify opinions. Each student is given a key word in a multi-stepped process (in this case, a river system). The student must then physically place the word in its appropriate order in the continuum and justify why it should be at this point.

It's last period Thursday. I'm behind in the curriculum with my Year 7 SOSE class. I have to find a way to moderate their need to have so many questions answered, to engage them in more PEEL activities and GET ON WITH THE COURSE! They file in—rowdy after their last class—but I'm not deterred. We have an activity to finish before we get onto the task I WANT to do this lesson.

We've been undertaking a study of 'the earth', but every topic we've discussed has taken twice as long as I anticipate. Their questions, dare I say, are driving me nuts, but I don't admit that to anyone—after all I'm supposed to be a PEEL teacher and questioning is what we want! I put an end to their never-ending questions about rivers by telling them we don't have time for any more questions right now; we have an activity we must complete this lesson.

We've talked about rivers, answered a million questions about rivers and completed the comprehension questions out of their compulsory text purchase. I want to try the river continuum—it's a hands-on activity. I'm tired of all the text-based work. I want the class to have fun with their learning. At last, my classroom will look like a real PEEL classroom—kids buzzing and total engagement.

I demand their attention.

'Listen carefully,' I say.

'I'm going to give everyone a card. On the card you will find a word which has something to do with a river system. Then we're all going to stand up and make a circle around the tables I've carefully arranged down the centre of the room. When I say! NOT NOW! When I tell you!'

I look to my folder for my cards—they've disappeared. I search frantically—more time wasted.

They're nowhere to be found. I throw a sheet of blank paper at each student as I rush around the room.

'I'm going to tell you what word to write as I come around, so listen carefully!' I splutter.

I hear from the far corner—the questions starting again:

'How do you spell DELTA?'

'I've got that word—why are you giving it to Simon?'

'How big does the writing have to be?'

'Can I use texta?'

I'm oblivious to all questions—I just want to complete this wonderfully PEELish activity. At last we have some sort of order and everyone has a card with a word related to rivers written on it . . . I hope that everyone can understand what the cards say—the spelling is atrocious.

Several hours later, or so it seems, the students are lined up around the table.

I start speaking. 'OK—this is how it works. We're going to start with Andrea. She's going to place her card on the table where she thinks it should go in a real river system; at the start, the end, or somewhere in the middle. Joanne will go next. (She's a bright girl so I know she'll do this well, I think to myself.) Joanne is going to place her card next and then we'll follow in order around the room. When Jo puts her card down she has to explain why she's put it there, why her part of the river system should go there. Everyone has to do the same. You can change the order of any card when it comes to your turn but you must justify the move.'

At the end of the tables, a few boys are pushing each other, another boy has sat down and the girls down the back are squirming restlessly. Joanne places her 'meander' card with a brilliant explanation. Mathew's next. He wants to pass. 'NO PASSING!' He places the card on the table with no justification other than 'that's where I want to put it'. This sets the scene for several others. A few of the students think carefully about where their cards should go and justify their choices admirably, but the majority of students are chatting to one another and moving as far away from the central tables as they can possibly get. We get almost to the last student when the bell rings. I believe I hear a sigh as students rush back to the safety of their own tables and begin to pack up.

What a disaster! I can't wait to get out of the room, out of the school. I don't ever want to see a continuum activity again. I leave the classroom thankful that this disaster is over. The sigh of relief now is my own. Tomorrow we can start something new and I won't ever have to think about this failure again. To add to my pain, I arrive back to my desk to find the brightly coloured, laminated, correctly spelled river systems cards in a neat pile. I talk to no one and get out of my staff room as fast as I can, defeated and deflated.

As I drive home, I start to cool off—it's a long drive. I can't help but reflect on the session and my own questioning process begins. It is a good procedure! Why didn't it work? By dinner I have a list of at least ten possible reasons.

I have the class first period the next morning and I start by telling them that I'd really like to do the continuum activity again. I think I detect groans from the back of the room but I swallow my pride and move on.

I explain why I want to give it another go: 'It's a great way for you to check your own understanding of river systems and especially to learn to justify your opinions.'

A hand shoots up. 'What does justify mean?'

We work out the meaning and I ask for further questions before we start.

'What's a billabong?'

'What's a riffle?'

'I'm not sure when the meander is eroded and when it deposits.'

'What does deposit mean?'

We run through all the terms in the continuum and I jot key words and meanings on the board for reference. Finally the class agrees that we will give the continuum another go.

We take our cards and sit in a circle on the floor at the back of the room. Everyone is looking pretty comfortable and relaxed. We establish some rules on talking during others' turns and clarify the fact that you can move any of the cards when it's your turn but you have to explain why you are doing it. You mustn't interrupt another person but you can have another turn second time around. I ask who would like to start. Surprisingly, several hands go up. The process begins slowly but students are aware of how the procedure should work and what their terms mean (the definitions are still on the board so they can refer to them if needed). We get to student six or seven and I detect some squirming again.

To my delight, I realise that it's not discomfort or lack of interest that's creating this movement. I see hands over several mouths as I realise that students are stopping themselves from interrupting other students' justifications. The squirming is now through enthusiasm and an eagerness to have another turn, or to change the order of the continuum. Students who rarely contribute in class are eager and even confident when it is their turn. Some place only their own card, but many challenge other students' opinions and move the continuum through their own justifications.

We're again close to finishing when the bell rings. Only four students stand up to leave! The eager eyes of each student are on their own card and where it's been moved to. Several students cannot contain themselves and take the bell as an opportunity to have their say. An argument ensues over the 'correct' order of the continuum. I placate further dispute by explaining that several orders can be correct and that it is the process of justification that is important. I congratulate the class on their best lesson of the year. They give themselves a rowdy round of applause and reluctantly leave for their next class.

In the next class we reflect on the previous lesson and I ask what they thought of the activity. I'm told:

'It was fun.'

'It's good having a chance to say what you think and to chal-
lenge other people.'
'It really helps you understand river systems.'
'It's good that you can have your say and argue your point.'

This *was* the best lesson I've had with this class. I felt like I could see
them learning—and I had been ready *never* to do the continuum
activity again after that first disaster. If I had not taken the risk, and
the challenge, to attempt the continuum again so much student
learning would never have occurred. All of what I had attempted to
achieve through introducing the L Files books would not have had a
chance to be reflected in this 'disaster'. What a lot I have to learn!

It is now the end of semester. Time to reconstruct our good
learners on butcher's paper. The students are told they cannot use
their L Files books as they break into their original groups. I'm
amazed at the results. I wonder if the students are 'teacher pleasing'
by drawing and writing what they know I'd like to see. Just six months
later, we had moved on from creating 'nice pictures' as our goal to
quite sophisticated explanations of a 'good learner'.

Figure 5.2: Good learner poster at the end of the semester

Has this been a result of remembering GLBs from the L Files books, or actually putting the GLBs into place through such activities as the continuum? Or has it been a mixture of both? Does an explanation of what a good learning behaviour is have to precede the experience of being involved in the GLBs or vice versa? This sounds like a good topic for teacher research.

REFLECTIONS

As I reflect on my research, I see that I have learnt much more than I ever anticipated. We have not used the L Files in any serious manner this term, yet students are still linking, questioning and self-monitoring.

There are many things that this first attempt at teacher research has taught me:

- I understand now that there are many facets to good teaching and of a PEEL lesson and that you cannot make a lesson successful, in terms of learning, unless you really do share some of the intellectual control with the students. Initially the students had seen no purpose in the continuum task (just as they had initially seen no purpose in the creation of posters showing a good learner). It was only once the students had a need to know that the real learning began. It was when they began questioning before we completed the second continuum that the students understood what the task was and how they were able to be productively involved. It was here that the real learning—the thinking—began.
- I know now that the questioning that I guiltily despised in the students was not the 'good' questioning that PEEL promotes and once again this became clear to me when students actually started asking meaningful questions relating to the second attempt at the continuum.
- I know that students (as I was told during a further discussion with the class on good learning) need to be told *how* to do something, not just *what* to do. I have learnt that there is often a disparity in what I think students understand and what they do understand

and that we, as teachers, should never make assumptions about student understanding—as I had in the first continuum.

- I've learnt how independent these students can be in their thinking, what good learners each of them can be, and that I should always have high expectations of them. Once again I was reminded of the importance of positive self-esteem in determining self-motivation and a positive attitude to learning—for both students and teachers.

- My expectations were that I would move the class on a steady path forward in their learning, that I would achieve a clear and decisive response to my research question, and that I would be able to clearly say that the students had become metacognitive. Of course I cannot say that I know that now, but I can say that they have certainly moved forward in their metacognitive processes and that metacognition has developed to varying degrees in individual students.

- I accept that I expected too much, too fast. Learning is ongoing— the GLBs need to be reinforced in an ongoing way, not learned by rote! The situation has to be experienced for it to be real and for it to have meaning to students. Just as I was able to learn from my own perceived 'disasters' by taking the risks associated with the procedure and activities I undertook with this class, so too students needed to learn from experience.

- In undertaking research, I have realised that once you begin considering learning along with teaching, it becomes clear that teaching and learning are not synonymous and that teachers, along with students, will always be challenged with, and by, learning. As a teacher, I will forever be challenged to take risks and ride the roller coaster of learning along with my students.

REFERENCES

Baird, J.R. and Northfield, J.R. (1992). *Learning from the PEEL Experience*. Melbourne: Monash University.

Mitchell, I.J. and Mitchell, J.A. (eds) (1997). *Stories of Reflective Teaching: A Book of PEEL Cases*. Melbourne: PEEL Publishing.

Swan, S. and White, R.T. (1994). *The Thinking Books*. London: Falmer Press.

White, R.T. and Gunstone, R.F. (1992). *Probing Understanding*. London: Falmer Press.

PART 3

Researching changes in learning

6

Linking: A strategy for enhancing learning

Pia Jeppersen

INTRODUCTION

Frustration of an experienced teacher

One of the most frustrating things for me as a Mathematics teacher is the way students compartmentalise ideas or methods in their minds and, unless an explicit attempt is made to retrieve them, they rarely use them again. Students generally do not make connections from topic to topic, lesson to lesson, or even between activities within a lesson. This has been a common thread in my PEEL group and in *PEEL SEEDS* (e.g. Di Mieri, 1993; Corkhill, 1995).

Mathematics contains much sequential content. For example, factorisation of quadratic trinomials requires an understanding of factorising linear expressions. This topic, in turn, requires the basic ideas of algebraic expansion and other associated algorithms. Given this, it should be relatively easy for a student to make connections to previous learning in Mathematics. It isn't. An added difficulty is that Mathematics is often perceived by students (and parents) to be the 'hardest and most important' school subject. As a result, students are often so preoccupied with passing that there seems to be little room left for anything else. The irony of this is that students do not seem to realise that reflection on their learning can help them to overcome these anxieties.

From frustration to research

My concerns eventually became a Masters research project. I set out to explore how I could encourage students in my Mathematics class to reflect on the connections and links in the content they were taught. An important intended outcome was to empower the students' learning through enhancing their sense of responsibility and control over it. I also hoped that, in the process, Mathematics would become more meaningful for them and that this would generate further interest in their responsibilities as active learners.

BACKGROUND

Some personal beliefs about teaching and learning

As a teacher, I aim to challenge the views that my students hold about their role in their learning. As part of my normal teaching practice, I try to communicate to them that I am interested in helping them learn 'how to learn'. I use everyday language to try to model or highlight good learning behaviours. For example, I encourage the students to seek help from each other before they seek help from me and I ask them to justify their responses to my questions. I have learnt that working in this way with students requires good rapport and a close working relationship.

I try to establish and maintain a supportive learning environment in which students are not afraid to take risks—in other words, one in which they feel comfortable with offering their own ideas and opinions, without the fear of being ridiculed. Establishing this environment requires me to model patience and respect and to have a clear expectation that the students will support each other's learning. For example, at the start of the year, students could generate a set of 'class rules' and 'Characteristics of a Good Teacher' (Jeppersen, 1993) with the expectation that they be observed for the remainder of the year. A considerable amount of time is spent on the students listening to each other's ideas about what 'learning' means to them. My students are challenged about their views of their responsibilities as learners and I encourage them to show initiative in the way in which the lessons/topics develop. This investment of time and energy usually has been successful in ensuring that some good learning happens.

The study's broad frames

Several ideas from the literature on metacognition, PEEL, other Masters theses and my own experience served as a springboard into the study. The various PEEL publications (e.g. Baird and Northfield, 1995; Mitchell and Mitchell, 1997), as well as the many PEEL meetings I have attended, suggested frames, strategies, techniques and ideas that promote 'good learning' and that encourage students to 'think about thinking'. Throughout the seven years prior to my study taking place, I had extensively trialled, refined and adapted these ideas to suit the needs of my students and the aims of my lessons. Many of these ideas had become a part of my teaching repertoire, occurring naturally and automatically.

The term metacognition is often used in conjunction with the idea of 'students taking responsibility for their own learning'. Metacognition can be broadly defined as thinking about one's own thoughts (Flavell, 1979). In the practical context of the classroom, metacognition includes the ability of the student to ask questions of the following type:

- What do I know about this topic/subject?
- Do I know where I can get some more information?
- What are some strategies I can use to learn this?
- Did I understand what I just learnt/heard/saw?
- How do I know if I have made a mistake? How do I find it?

Bakapanos (1988) and Macdonald (1990) concluded that a change in how students think about thinking can only occur when the students actually see the value in investing energy in order to lead to change. Therefore, students need opportunities to practise these new skills and learn about their particular learning style in order to accomplish the desired change. When I read about these ideas, they struck a chord with me and helped to shape the initial direction of my study.

One of my broad themes was to explore the nature of student change. More specifically, I aimed to see whether, and how, students' perceptions of their roles in their own learning would change over the course of the year whilst I was purposely developing their linking skills. To try to achieve this change, the students were encouraged to share ownership of how the class ran. They worked together with a common focus, 'the class goal'. Activities centred on making connections or links between techniques, concepts and topics. It follows that student and teacher reflection formed a crucial part of these activities.

The study also drew on published teaching principles and learning behaviours to provide a more specific focus. Firstly, two of the twelve Principles of Teaching for Quality Learning (Mitchell and Mitchell, 1997) which relate to student change were relevant:

- Principle 10: Develop student awareness of the big picture: how the various activities fit together and link to the big idea; and
- Principle 11: Regularly raise student awareness of the nature of the components of quality learning.

Secondly, two of the Poor Learning Tendencies (Baird and White, 1982) were important in terms of reflective thought:

- lack of internal reflective thinking; and
- lack of external reflective thinking,

Finally, the Good Learning Behaviours (GLBs) described behaviours that I wished to promote:

- GLB 12: seeks links between adjacent activities and ideas; and,
- GLB 13: seeks links between non-adjacent activities, ideas and between different topics (Baird and Northfield, 1992).

AIMS OF THE STUDY

The original aims of the study were as follows:

- To what extent do specific teaching procedures (Thinking Books, Topic Linkup, class discussion and T-Cards) enhance student awareness of the importance of making links and the learning strategies involved when making links?
- Does the incidence of linking increase over the year of intervention?
- To what extent are students making links with respect to:
  - links between concepts within a mathematical topic and from topic to topic; and,
  - links between algorithms within a mathematical topic and from topic to topic.

It seemed obvious to me that the students' attitude to learning and their perceptions of their role in their own learning would significantly affect the progress of them making successful links. Therefore, I proposed that, when linking occurs, it might be able to be classified as one of three levels: guided, reflective or automatic linking.

Guided linking

If a student was working on a particular idea, the teacher might guide the student to a better understanding through questioning directed at the student making links to previous knowledge. For example, questions such as 'Yesterday we did an activity on the same ideas. Can you write down three similarities between yesterday's work and today's work?' would promote guided linking.

Reflective linking

The student may make links when invited or encouraged to do so by the teacher or other students. This does involve some teacher facilitation, but not to the same extent as in guided linking. A typical facilitating statement could be 'Yesterday's work and today's work share some similarities. Can you think of any other examples in which you will find the same methods being used?'

Automatic linking

Students may make links between the task at hand and other beliefs or knowledge without teacher or peer prompt or intervention.

At the conclusion of the study, the aims listed above were not fully addressed. However, this was not an unexpected outcome as I was intent on the classroom events dictating the direction of the study, rather than the other way around. I found that I was documenting other valuable changes in my class. The concept of linking was central to the study, but the focus gradually moved from linking, and how it could be used to enhance quality learning, to the bigger picture of students' expectations of their own, and their teacher's, role in learning mathematics.

CONTEXTUAL FACTORS

The study was conducted at an independent girls' school. Most of the students were from upper socio-economic backgrounds. The sample class, which varied from fifteen to twenty students, consisted of students in Year 8 (aged thirteen to fourteen years).

Mathematics classes at the school were grouped according to ability level, and this sample class was Band 2 of Bands 1 to 3. They were generally not creative thinkers in Mathematics; however, they were keen learners and would usually tackle a task with motivation and purpose. Throughout my teaching, I did not deviate from the full Year 8 Mathematics curriculum.

The physical setting of the classroom was integral to establishing a supportive work environment. I was allocated the same room for all my classes, and this allowed my students and me to 'own' the room.

THE INTERVENTION

Laying the foundations for good learning to occur

I did not introduce my major focus on linking, nor start formal data collection, until the second term of a four-term year. During Term 1, I drew on my previous experiences in PEEL to prepare the class for the more formal research. The first lesson of the year was crucial to my strategy for encouraging in students a sense of respect for each other, for our learning environment and for promoting an agenda of learning. The students filled in a communication sheet (Figure 6.1) and its questions provided starting points for discussion of mathematical and academic interests, weaknesses and strengths as well as long- and short-term goals. The students also considered the reasons for attending school, their long-term career aspirations, and their views about parental influence on their education.

During the remainder of Term 1, I taught the set curriculum. When and where appropriate, I discussed and demonstrated (or modelled) various learning strategies with the students. For example, students were encouraged to seek help from their peers before asking me and, after initial encouragement from me, this occurred routinely. I used a number of PEEL teaching procedures (Baird and Northfield, 1992):

- building on old procedures;
- comments on comments;
- students selecting their own problems;
- encouraging students to admit to not understanding; and,
- building on student misconceptions.

The students became familiar with these procedures and appeared to enjoy using them.

By the end of Term 1, I felt that I had developed a good rapport with students, with more than half the class willing to 'take risks'. We had established, for example, that all questions were 'good' questions, that no 'put-downs' were allowed, and that homework was usually defined as what each student could achieve in 20 minutes of solid work. The students discovered that I was willing to listen to and use

Year 8 Communication Sheet   **Name:**

1. Were you in Junior School? If so, how many years were you there?
2. Which Band were you in last year and which Maths teacher did you have?
3. Please fill in the following on the continuum below:
   a) your favourite subject
   b) your least favourite subject
   c) where Maths fits on the continuum

0   5   10

least favourite   most favourite

4. Please give a number for each of the following (0 = not at all, 10 = definitely!).
   a) I enjoy Maths   b) I am good at Maths
   c) I find Maths easy   d) I ask questions when I am stuck
5. How do you prefer working? Please circle your preference. Individually, in pairs, in small groups of three or four, as a large class group
6. Think back to last year. How well do you think you did your homework? Were you happy with your homework efforts? Would you change anything about the way you did your homework?
7. What is your personal goal for Maths this term?
8. What is your personal goal for Maths this year?
9. What is your favourite treat?
10. Can you tell me something about what your parents' expectations are of you with regard to Maths and how well you do in this subject?

Figure 6.1: Communication sheet

their ideas in the lesson. Even at this early stage in the year, students were demonstrating a range of good learning behaviours. For example, students were asking me 'Why they went wrong', telling me 'what they didn't understand', asking each other for help before they asked me, 'checking my work for errors and offering corrections', and 'justifying opinions' (as per some of the GLBs in Baird and Northfield, 1992). The students were engaged in their learning and were responding positively and constructively to the opportunity to be part of the decision-making processes of the lessons. We had also identified 'experts' in various topics within the class who had been able to help their peers.

Establishing the class goal

At the start of Term 2, I felt that the class was ready to start the formal research. I wanted to introduce the students to both the notion of the 'big picture'—that is, the links between the topics across the whole year—and the notion of them taking a very real responsibility for their learning over the whole year.

Questions 7 and 8 in Figure 6.1 were used as starting points in establishing our class goal for the year. Students were eager to share their responses with the rest of the class and rich discussion ensued. Not surprisingly, a common theme was 'to improve'. We also discussed the difference between learning something just to get it right on a test and learning with understanding. Students noted that good grades on a test or an assignment did not necessarily mean that they could explain concepts and techniques to another person or that they had developed an appropriate understanding of the work. We ended this discussion by agreeing that our class goal should be 'to improve in our understanding and standard of Maths'.

The students' comments indicated a perception that the teacher held all the answers. This perception provided an excellent starting point for exploring what the students perceived to be their and my roles in their learning. Using a communication sheet, I asked the students to complete the following three statements.

Statement 1:   To understand something means . . .

Statement 2:   Learning is about . . .

Statement 3:   Learning Maths is about . . .

I stressed that there were no right or wrong answers; rather, I was interested in their opinions. The responses to these statements were diverse and sophisticated. For example:

Statement 1:   To understand something means . . .

- something is very clear to you and you know what it means;
- to absorb information that you can use when needed.

Statement 2:   Learning is about . . .

- preparation for a future career;
- discovering new things and new ideas and storing them in our mind for when we need to use them;
- helping us to understand all the different familiar things around us and changes that occur in our environment, whether it's at school or at home.

Statement 3:   Learning Maths is about . . .

- learning formulas and counting and things that will help you get a job and go to university;
- learning about basic skills to make our day-to-day life easier.

Understanding means . . .
- That you know what something means
- You have it in your mind
- You know it very well and you feel confident with it
- To learn something
- You know what people say to you
- Understanding what you are doing after you understand what you understand
- Knowing what to do to get the right answer, etc. in the situation you are in.

Figure 6.2: Understanding poster

Learning is about . . .
- Knowing things that you don't know
- Discovering new things and new ideas and storing them in our minds for when we need to use them
- Getting to know what is going on around us
- Being able to support yourself
- Gathering information
- Discovering a new thing or a different to way to do something
- Absorbing information so that we can use it in the future
- Preparation for a future career
- Really thinking about things
- Knowing how or what to do in association with the thing that you are talking about

Figure 6.3: Learning poster

I collated the students' responses to Statements 1 and 2, placed them on posters and pinned them on to one of the noticeboards in our classroom (see Figures 6.2 and 6.3).

Our class goal is:
To improve in our understanding and in our standard of Maths
How are we going to do this?
More study
Work harder
Improve our memories
Ask lots of questions
How can we improve our memories?
More exercises/practice
Playing games to learn
Writing things down
Music in working time—Handel, Bach, Mozart
Thinking about the different things and how they are related
Let's call this last sentence 'Linking'

Figure 6.4: Class goal

I used these two posters as a starting point for brainstorming and discussion on how the students would collaboratively achieve our class goal. The students' ideas were then used to construct a third poster (Figure 6.4).

These three posters became effective and concrete ways of reminding the students about their commitment to taking responsibility for their own learning. The third poster was particularly effective in helping students to reflect on their progress in working towards the class goal.

The use of specific linking procedures

I spent the next three terms teaching the set curriculum using a wide range of learning procedures. Class discussion was integral to all lessons, stimulating students to make links and promoting student reflection. I also regularly used 'Thinking Books' (Swan and White, 1994), and two activities that I had developed, 'Topic Linkup' and 'T-Cards', specifically to enhance linking.

Discussion

Discussion encouraged careful listening and was the ideal forum for the development and refinement of ideas. I often taught a new concept or technique starting with the students' prior knowledge (linking the old ideas to the new ideas), and guided their learning with a series of questions. When it was appropriate and possible to follow up discussion with written reflection, I set aside five minutes in class or homework time for the students to write a personal paragraph summarising what we had discussed. I used statements such as 'Write down two more examples of where we would use this type of Maths when we are at home' or 'Write down three things that link with yesterday's discussion'. The students recorded their ideas in their thinking books. Mistakes or incorrect working also provided a focal point for more discussion, and comparisons enabled further links to be drawn.

Thinking Books

The importance of private communication with the individual student cannot be under-estimated and Thinking Books helped address this need. They were exercise books that I distributed part-way through the year. Their use varied—time was either allocated in class or for homework to write in the books. Sometimes I asked specific questions, sometimes I did not. Often, I would ask the students to reflect upon comments/ideas that had been recorded earlier. I collected the books at appropriate times and responded to their comments. At one student's suggestion, the linking activities that we did (e.g. brainstorming and concept mapping) were also recorded in the thinking books.

Topic Linkup

I developed this procedure to allow the students to see the whole of the course mapped out—to see the 'big picture'—and to encourage them to make links between the topics. The headings of each topic to be studied during the year were printed on sixteen blue A4 sheets. These were pinned at the back of the room (Figure 6.5), starting from the first topic in the left-hand top corner and working in an anti-clockwise direction.

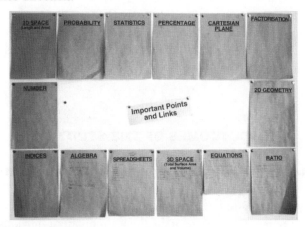

Figure 6.5: Topic Linkup

The Topic Linkup was used in many ways (e.g. as a review or brain-storming exercise at the start or end of a topic) and the students were generally enthusiastic, adding many new links to the cards. Some-times the students would suggest a new link, at other times I needed to ask a question such as 'Where have we used this type of working before?' I encouraged the students to think about examples and counter-examples to support their statements.

T-Cards (Thinking Cards)

I developed T-Cards (office index cards) for the students to use as a method for recording automatic linking quickly and easily. I explained that the purpose of the cards was to practise making links. I pointed out that sometimes if a student thought of a link and did not write it down it could 'become lost', particularly if it was not appropriate to mention the link at that moment in the lesson. T-Cards also provided a more private way of recording ideas. Students were asked to record the date, the topic and the link on their card. I encouraged the students to write on the cards at any time throughout the lesson. I also encouraged them to then share their thoughts with a neighbour or with the rest of the class. Often I would ask for 'T-Card links' as part of the general discussion at the end of a lesson. On occasions, I would provide a few minutes in class for the students to privately record any links which had been made during a lesson. This would be followed by voluntary discussion. I also encouraged the students to use them during homework time.

OUTCOMES OF THE STUDY

Changes in student awareness of quality learning

As the year progressed, the students became more confident learners and more aware of the nature of quality learning. It was obvious to me that they felt comfortable with sharing their ideas as they were secure in the knowledge that they would be taken seriously and that their ideas would be valued.

> We are relaxed and we are not scared to ask you questions.

They seemed to recognise that, to become more effective learners, they needed to be taking a more active role in their own learning. By the end of the year, the students were willing to help make decisions on the direction of a lesson or topic. Occasionally they would compare the way in which this year's Maths classes ran with their (not so satisfactory) experiences from last year's Maths classes. The end result was that, as the students experienced success, there was an increase in their interest in both Mathematics and the learning that was taking place.

General student reflections on the value of linking and the usefulness of the activities in promoting linking

At the end of Term 3, I asked the students to respond to a communication sheet which focused on the ideas of linking and the activities used in promoting linking. They thought that linking was a valuable part of the learning process and that the activities that we had used had been useful in helping them make links:

> Linking is important for our learning because if you understand one topic, you may not know much about another topic but if you link one thing to another, then you might realise what the topic is all about.

> Linking can be important, 'cos it can help you to remember things but I don't usually use it.

> The activities have helped me to think more about the links between ideas and topics because now when I get a new subject I think about what the subject's about.

The activities have helped, they make you understand more.

The linking activities have helped because I listen more in discussions.

At this stage in the year, the students certainly *had* developed a sense of the network of links between different topics. The Topic Linkup and related teaching strategies were successful in encouraging this awareness of the big picture. Their ability to independently link the different topics was uneven; however, the students were able to clearly express their views on the usefulness of each of the activities in promoting their *awareness* of linking and they were willing to suggest improvements to them. Most importantly, with prompting, the students were able to justify their reasons—this showed their understanding of linking and how it had been useful. For me, this mature level of thinking was an impressive outcome.

From my observation and the students' comments on the various activities, class discussion seemed to be most valued by the students for exploring the ideas of learning and how understanding could be enhanced through making connections. It was easy, involved a minimum amount of 'written thinking' and a lot of ideas could be exchanged in a short time:

With discussion, you can ask a question and get an answer straight away, but if you write a question, it takes a long time and talking is fun!

The students were ambivalent about the use of the Thinking Books—probably partly due to their inconsistent use as a result of 'too many things happening':

Thinking books have been useful because you can ask questions and not get embarrassed and we don't use them very much and I think that thinking books may be useful but I am not sure how to use them.

Initially, students enjoyed using the Topic Linkup to record their ideas on linking. The activity seemed to be successful in promoting awareness of the 'big picture' and how the various topics fitted together.

> I think that talking about things and doing the blue sheets—
> umm—important points and links thing, has made me think
> more about linking.

However, their interest waned as the year progressed:

> It slows discussion down when we have to stop so that we can
> write it on the sheets.

From my own observations, the students gained more from the Topic Linkup than they realised, as they were able to offer constructive criticism for its improvement in subsequent years. However, they did not embrace the use of the T-Cards. They could not see value in using them and therefore were reluctant to expend the energy to explore how they could be used:

> Even though I have thought of something, I wouldn't write it
> down.

The students seemed to enjoy the novelty of having a teacher who wanted them to 'have a say' in the overall direction of the year. They obviously felt valued as individuals and took the responsibilities that were offered them seriously:

> I like the way we work because it lets us decide on how we
> want to do things and it is our fault if we don't get things done
> or if we don't ask for help.

One student commented to her friend:

> It's good that she doesn't get angry if we don't like doing some-
> thing.

The friend replied:

Yeah, I wish our other teachers were the same.

Interestingly, in general, the stronger and more confident Mathematics students were more comfortable with being part of the decision-making process than the weaker, less confident students. I found that I needed to monitor this balance very closely.

In previous years, I had not established a class goal. When comparing this class with my previous years' classes, it was obvious to me that the common goal had helped to focus students and create an atmosphere of 'learning together':

> The class are all really cooperative and we all get along. Nobody hates each other.

It also resulted in students appreciating that everyone was able to contribute:

> If you don't understand something people try to explain it to you.

> We are *never* scared to ask questions and we support each other.

Furthermore, the goal gave students an immediate sense of responsibility for the direction that the year would take and a real commitment to the important role that they—individually and collectively—had to play in achieving their goal. The main problem with having the year-long class goal was that students 'switched off' in the last part of the year. Possibly there were too many agenda for the students to follow. They were being challenged to work cooperatively, to work to achieve their personal goals, perhaps to become accustomed to a different style of teaching, to take an active responsibility for their learning and to think about thinking. It was no wonder they were exhausted by the end of the year!

Overloading students with 'all this thinking'

It was important to let the ideas and the processes of learning take shape slowly. However, despite my good intentions, halfway through

Term 4 students pointed out that they felt overloaded. It was a significant achievement in itself that they could identify that they *had* been learning about learning. The students indicated that, at this stage in the year, they wanted a more traditional 'chalk and talk' method of teaching, claiming that they felt quite tired from 'all this talk'. In response, I agreed to teach a more traditional lesson. The result provided some very important and unexpected data.

Teacher: OK—so you've told me that you are tired of us talking about learning. Would you like me to try to teach this lesson in a 'chalk and talk' way?

What do you mean?

Teacher: Well, it means that I stand out the front here and I will teach you today's lesson, which is the start of factorisation, our new topic. If you are to pretend to be 'traditional students' then you are not allowed to ask any questions until I ask you if you have any and all you do is copy down the work and do as I say. Are you ready?

Yeah.

(I write the topic on the board, then write a definition of factorisation and four simple examples with answers.)

[In background] Do you understand what she is doing?

No—but we are not allowed to ask her.

I don't understand this, Miss Jepp.

Teacher: Shhh! Just write this down and then I will explain.

(I then write six other examples with answers on the board and then wait a few minutes for all the students to finish writing. I notice that a few students are trying to make sense of the algorithms.)

Teacher: Stop talking please and sit quietly until everyone is finished.

We were just trying to work things out.

Teacher: There is no need to do that—I will explain it once everyone is finished.

(I wait a minute longer and then ask for 'pens down, eyes up'. I go through each question, asking closed questions such as: What is a factor? What is the highest common factor of $8a$ and $12b$?

What is left behind when I take out a factor of 4? Several students have their hands raised apparently to ask rather than answer questions. I ignore them until I have finished all questions and then address these students.)

Teacher: Yes?

I understand Questions 1 to 4 but I don't get Question 5.

(There are murmurs from others in the class. I explain again how to solve the question. At this stage, there are two small groups of students who are helping each other work through the questions.)

Teacher: The students who are not listening! When I am talking, you listen! You might learn something and then you won't need to be distracting the rest of the class!

But we were just trying to work it out for ourselves.

Teacher: Listen first and then come and see me if you are still stuck.

(Having explained Question 5, I then ask if there are any other questions, and wait for one second—a short wait-time for me. I then start to write some exercises on the board, instructing the students to write them down and then to do them. While I am doing this, one student calls out).

Miss Jepp, can we try and make some questions up for ourselves?

Teacher: No—why would you want to do that? Do the exercises that I have set you. And I think that we will work in silence today.

(At this point, one of the students speaks up. My attempt at teaching a more 'traditional chalk and talk lesson' and expecting the students to be 'traditional learners' lasted only ten minutes!)

Miss Jepp, do we have to keep doing this? Every time we want to ask you a question or work something out with a friend you tell us off—when usually you want us to ask questions and talk to our friends!

(From the students' comments, it was obvious that they did not like me doing this.)

Teacher: What do the rest of you think? Do you want me to stop teaching you like this?

Yes!

Teacher: Why?
Because it's boring!
We like being able to work things out for ourselves.
We want to ask you for help when we need it.
I want to try to make up some really hard questions.

This impromptu activity was a powerful means of highlighting both to the students and me how much they were doing now as independent learners. We realised that they were using thinking and linking skills that they had learnt throughout the year and that they could not revert to passive learning.

Changes in perceptions of performance

In the final lesson of the year, the students were given back the communication sheet that they had filled out in the first lesson. They were asked to reflect on what they had written and then to 're-answer' these initial questions in a different coloured pen. Twelve of the original seventeen students responded.

A comparison of the changes in their responses to Question 4 (Table 6.1) provided evidence that there had been a change in students' general attitudes and perceptions of performance.

All but two students recorded a change in some of their responses. Class discussion revealed student agreement that, as the year progressed, they became more confident with themselves as learners, and were more willing to help make decisions on the direction of a lesson or topic.

The students then responded to a new set of questions reflecting on their learning experiences over the year. One question was: 'Do you think that you have improved in your standard of Maths this year? Try and give a reason for this?' Nine of the twelve students who responded felt that they had improved:

I think I have improved in my standard of Maths this year because I like your style of teaching. But overall I like how Maths is taught. You just need good teachers.

I think I have improved in my standard of work *not* because of the work, but because of the teacher we had—who actually listened, helped and cared for us.

I think that my standard has improved because of the effort that I have put in and the helpful guidance we have had.

In summary, I was able to change how the students learned and how they believed they should learn and this led to increased confidence in their performance in Mathematics.

Table 6.1:   Changes in scores for Question 4

Question 4: Please give a number for each of the following (0 = not at all, and 10 = definitely).

a) I enjoy Maths   b) I am good at Maths
c) I find Maths easy   d) I ask questions when I am stuck

	Same score	Higher score	Lower score
a) I enjoy Maths	6	6	0
b) I am good at Maths	5	6	1
c) I find Maths easy	3	7	2
d) I ask questions when I am stuck	5	6	1
Total (n = 48 responses)	**19**	**25**	**4**

PERSONAL REFLECTIONS

I had set out to promote linking, and had some real success, but the changes in this area were only a part of the substantial changes in how the students learned. Good learning has a number of interconnected aspects and, as I found, it is not possible to explore one without also developing the others.

This study added a new dimension to the way in which I reflected on and approached my teaching. It meant that, in addition to thinking about the issues of learning associated with each topic, I formally reflected on a particular aspect of quality learning (linking) as well as the overall direction of the whole year. This shift in my focus directly impacted on how the students responded to my teaching and thus on their reflection on their learning. The main differences between this class and classes that I had taught in previous years with a general focus of teaching for quality learning were:

* I was better able to harness and maintain the interest levels of the students;
* stronger teacher-student rapport;
* more stable class dynamics, with all students feeling comfortable with taking risks; and,
* I was more systematic and purposeful in promoting quality learning and more students displayed characteristics of independent learning.

This study has clearly shown me that students can be mature and confident thinkers and learners and that teachers do students a disservice if they do not provide opportunities for them to be responsible for taking a major part in their own learning.

REFERENCES

Baird, J.R. and Northfield, J.R. (eds) (1992). *Learning from the PEEL Experience*. Melbourne: PEEL Publishing.

Baird, J.R. and White, R.T. (1982). Promoting Self-control of Learning. *Instructional Science*, 11, 227–47.

Bakopanos, V. (1988). Encouraging Reflective Thinking in an Upper Secondary Classroom. Unpublished Masters Thesis.

Corkhill, P. (1995). PEELing Maths at Frankston High School. *PEEL SEEDS*, 29, 1–3.

Di Mieri, S. (1993). PEEL in LOTE: Linking. *PEEL SEEDS*, 22, 38–9.

Flavell, J.H. (1979). Metacognition and Cognitive Monitoring: A New Area of Cognitive-Developmental Inquiry. *American Psychologist*, 34, 906–11

Jeppersen, P. (1993). Student Generated Class Rules. *PEEL SEEDS*, 23, 17.

Macdonald, I. (1990). Student Awareness of Learning. Unpublished Masters Thesis.

Swan, S.M. and White, R.T. (1994). *The Thinking Books*. London: Falmer Press.

7

Do assessment practices match teaching strategies?

Jo Kindred and David Burke
with Tim Stephens and Rhonda Colley

This chapter describes both individual journeys and a group journey.

BACKGROUND

David: I tried a different approach with a Science test that focused almost solely on interpretation/analysis of graphs/tables/diagrams. Most middle-performing boys gained the best results while most top-performing girls actually dropped in achievement. This led me to the question of whether successes (and the resultant awards) go to well-behaved, neat, articulate students who respond better on the more conventional assessment tasks. It also led me to question what is it we teachers actually assess. How often do we assess and formally value good learning behaviours such as cooperative learning, questioning/listening skills and linking, or the higher order skills of Bloom's Taxonomy (Bloom, 1956) or Multiple Intelligences (Gardner, 1983)?

To explore this issue, we established a research team of two staff members—David, an Assistant Principal, and Jo, an English/SOSE/ Drama contract teacher. We were concerned about students' motivation and achievement, partly due to the familiar sight at the College's Presentation Night each year of a poor number of Year 9 students on stage collecting academic awards and, in particular, the lack of boys on stage representing the middle school. Each year, girls in Years 9 and 10 collected the most awards and had their participation in extra-curricular activities acknowledged. There was a message for us in this under-representation: not only did boys not achieve, but they did not really involve themselves in ways that could be described as 'having a go'.

PEEL has a ten-year history at our secondary college, but we were concerned that many teachers, while encouraging students to adopt good learning behaviours in the classroom, were not following this through to its natural conclusion—assessment of those behaviours. We suspected that this decline in learning, particularly amongst boys, was influenced by what teachers were assessing. It seemed to us that assessment was often too narrow when compared to the outcomes, skills and abilities that students were expected to learn and develop and, as a result, students were choosing to opt out of their learning. It follows that if teachers are to motivate students, they must broaden the nature of their assessment to include assessment of the learning behaviours that they value in the classroom.

Our final story as a result of examining these issues was threefold. Our research was firstly a journey of process. We encountered many problems along the way that reframed our thinking about ways to collect and use data. It was also a journey about assessment and students' perceptions about what assessment teachers value in the classroom. Finally, it was a journey about the effect our research had on ourselves and other members of staff. We arrived, eventually, at two main conclusions: that students have clear views about the nature of teaching and assessment that is valued in their classrooms; and that action research is fluid, changing and at times highly frustrating, but is also influential and often brings unexpected benefits.

DATA COLLECTION

Central to the project was the question: 'What do teachers value in assessment at Year 9 level?' We planned to investigate three aspects of assessment: an analysis of assessment tasks; what teachers valued; and what students valued in terms of assessment in the classroom. Jo began to approach some staff members (one Year 9 teacher from each Key Learning Area) for copies of tests/assignments/projects/work sheets they had used in their Year 9 classes, so these could be analysed. She found that most staff were extremely reluctant to hand over copies of their work. One senior Maths teacher even commented: 'I don't really want to give you this. It's really boring. Can't I give you something from Year 10 instead?' The request was clearly threatening for some staff, but we were surprised to find that access to colleagues' work, and hence to their classrooms, was restricted. We recognised that this represented a risk that many were unprepared to take.

We realised that if we were to collect data in this sensitive area, we would need more active staff involvement and ownership, with teachers involved in the process from the start—especially in terms of planning where and how the project should be developed. We envisaged the project having positive outcomes whereby staff involved would gain knowledge and help in improving and enriching their assessment practices—both at the Year 9 level and eventually across the whole school curriculum. In so doing, their early fears about the project might also be diminished. Unfortunately, when we approached staff about being involved, we received a lacklustre response from almost everyone. Few, it seemed, had the time.

It quickly became apparent that we had 'bitten off more than we could chew'. Finding time to conduct our research was also a big problem for us. We needed to contract to something that would be less threatening for other staff and more manageable for us. After much negotiation, we settled on investigating 'What do students think teachers value through assessment?'—one aspect of our initial plan. In spite of these problems, this first stage in our project was crucial because it provided us with an initial direction and focus and alerted us to some of the real problems facing researchers about process.

We tried various approaches to collecting data about what students thought teachers valued through assessment and eventually developed a student raw data record sheet through which students could do their own analysis of their assessment tasks. This data was to be accompanied by a 21-question interview with the students. After conducting eight interviews and writing up eight transcripts, we came to the conclusion that conducting this research and working full-time was too difficult. We decided to ask a part-time teacher, Tim Stephens, to join the research team.

Tim: I was very interested in this type of project. My first task for the project was to conduct the interviews, freeing up Jo and David to analyse the results. The more interviews I did, however, the more obvious it seemed to me that I was not getting the total story from the students. I saw this as a sign that the students were reluctant to criticise a teacher in front of me. No matter how many times or in how many ways I stressed the confidentiality of our discussions, I could not break through the barrier that I sensed was there. These students always saw me as a teacher, not an impartial researcher. The barrier remained until Rhonda arrived.

Tim's input was extremely valuable. In order to overcome the teacher-as-interviewer barriers that Tim had identified, the team used PAVOT funds to employ a parent, Rhonda, to conduct the student interviews.

Rhonda: I became involved with this project using spare time from my half-time position as an integration aide at the local primary school. I enjoyed working with the students and developed a good relationship with all of those I interviewed. Interviewing pairs of students was incredibly time-consuming. In using the sheet of questions and audio equipment to record responses, I took approximately 40 minutes for each interview and two hours to transcribe them. The tape recorder made some students feel uneasy and a little intimidated, but most students were able to cope very well with this form of interviewing. Not being a teacher at the college certainly helped me to obtain honest and accurate data. Some of the students' responses were very interesting, and some were quite amazing, considering their level of maturity as Year 9 students. I actually gained valuable information on different teaching strategies that I could implement into my integration work. Being involved in this project, and working with a wonderful, devoted team of teachers, has been an experience I will always appreciate.

At this point, we were able to refine our approach. The current process was providing good material but the interviews were taking too long and some of the questions were leading the students. However, the students' responses to these initial 21 questions were extremely useful in streamlining our approach. David developed an interview record tick sheet based on the responses to the interviews by Jo, Tim and Rhonda. Categories were developed to classify the students' responses. For example, for Question 1, 'How did your teacher go about teaching this topic?' the students gave responses such as:

The teacher just taught us.

We did group work.

We discussed it.

We did research.

We did activities or work sheets.

The teacher did an example for us.

These responses were then developed into categories: teacher taught; groups; discussion; research/investigation; activities/work sheets; modelling; and an 'other' category to cover responses that had yet to be raised. We found that we could collapse the original 21 questions into six new ones that covered the same ground.

We also agreed that it was possible for the same response to be recorded in more than one category. Using the tick sheet to record responses proved to be more user-friendly for all of us and was certainly less time consuming—an important issue.

Once again, although frustrating, this refocusing and re-setting of both goals and questions was important, as it moulded the four researchers together and helped us form a cohesive team with a common purpose.

> *Tim*: At this stage of the project I felt a real sense of ownership. The project almost seemed to be starting again from my point of view. The meetings where the team evaluated and reflected on their progress were amazingly useful as they gave me a chance to hear and discuss the goals of the project with all members of the team. As always seems to be the case, the best and most valuable meetings are those where small groups of interested teachers get together and talk about just that— teaching.

Over a period of several months, Rhonda interviewed 150 Year 9 students (in pairs) about recently completed assessment tasks in Maths or English using the interview record sheet we had developed. Assessment tasks included assignments/projects (seven), oral work (two), homework (one) and tests (two). Students were asked six questions:

- How did your teacher go about teaching you this unit?
- What did the assessment task indicate to you that the teacher wanted you to learn?
- What other skills did the teacher want you to learn?
- How do you know the teacher valued these skills?
- If you were the teacher, how would you go about teaching this topic?
- If you were the teacher, how would you go about assessing this topic?

The students' responses were categorised on the spot, but Rhonda was able to check what the students meant to ensure that all the responses in any one category matched our meaning for that category. As Rhonda noted, conducting successful interviews using the tick sheet was much simpler.

> *Rhonda*: It was taking so long to do the interviews and then transcribe them that I was really pleased with the tick sheet. I no longer had to find a room where I could set up a tape recorder and microphone. I could do the interviews anywhere, any time. In fact, some of the interviews took place sitting on the steps outside the student's classroom. The students also seemed to be more relaxed as there was no microphone and therefore they were more responsive to the questions asked. I found generally that their responses tended to neatly fit into the categories on the sheet. This is hardly surprising since the tick sheet had been developed using the student responses we already had. If their response didn't clearly match a category, I would question them further until we reached some consensus with the tick sheet. Of course, certain responses could fit into more than one category. For example, in response to Question 1, 'How did your teacher go about teaching you this unit?', students often replied: 'The teacher taught us and we had a discussion about it', a response which would automatically be recorded in both the 'teacher taught' and 'discussion' categories. After conducting a few interviews, I became quite skilled at interpreting student responses and recording them appropriately. I was also careful to record the comments students made if I felt they were relevant to our research and reflective of students' attitudes towards assessment.

STUDENT DATA: RESULTS

The students' responses (summarised in Appendix 7.1) were very interesting, particularly in light of some of the differences they highlighted between Maths and English. Students reported that their teachers used a range of teaching strategies (Question 1). Given the college's strong commitment towards the value of cooperative learning, far less group work was identified than we expected and group work was not identified as a learning strategy at all in English. The data on modelling are probably the least reliable, as many students indicated this took place as teacher-directed learning.

The students' perceptions of what their teachers wanted them to learn (Question 2) varied markedly between Maths and English—Maths students strongly believed assessment tasks indicated teachers valued:

- content and knowledge (18 per cent compared with English 1 per cent);
- problem-solving skills (21 per cent compared with English 0 per cent); and,
- comprehension and understanding (25 per cent compared with English 11 per cent).

On the other hand, in English, assessment tasks indicated to the students that teachers wanted to assess their ability to interpret and analyse information (40 per cent compared with Maths 0 per cent). Both English and Maths assessment tasks indicated to students that teachers highly valued the acquisition of skills (32 per cent for both subjects).

Students also indicated that different assessment tasks showed the teacher valued different skills at different times. Homework was seen to be valuing content and knowledge (54 per cent) with tests and projects valuing this same skill far less, at 7 per cent and 5 per cent respectively. General skills acquisition was spread fairly evenly across tests, projects and homework, but skills in interpretation were only valued in projects. Problem-solving, as well as comprehension, was valued mostly in tests and projects, but not in homework. Research skills, presentation and the ability to make links were seen to be of little importance in any assessment tasks in either English or Maths.

Questions 3 and 4 explored whether assessment practices matched teaching strategies. The students identified a range of (generally) non-assessed skills as being valued by their teachers. Listening skills (32 per cent) and on-task work (20 per cent) were seen as highly valued in both subjects, but unfortunately we did not probe sufficiently at the time to determine whether good listening skills referred to listening to the teacher, to each other, or both. Interestingly, cooperative learning skills were more highly valued in Maths (17 per cent compared with English 4 per cent). This was also true for good questioning skills (17 per cent in Maths compared with 11 per cent in English).

> *Rhonda*: The college has placed a priority on cooperative learning and table-groups were mentioned several times with comments about their composition. Some students felt that groups should be made up with two bright students helping two that were struggling. Others commented that groups should be all the same level, with brighter students given extra work to go on with, allowing the teacher more time to spend with the groups that were having difficulties with a particular topic.

When students were questioned about how they knew the teacher valued other skills, 53 per cent of students (67 per cent in English and 38 per cent in Maths) simply said the teacher told them or that they 'just knew they were'. Twenty-four per cent of students said their teacher praised them for their use of these skills and 10 per cent used their teacher's mood as a guide for their success in attaining these learning behaviours.

Maths teachers used more praise (33 per cent) compared with English (16 per cent) and showed more variation in mood (13 per cent) compared with English (6 per cent). Not surprisingly, responses here varied greatly from teacher to teacher. The interviews showed the importance of the teacher's mood.

> *Rhonda*: Students do pick up on the teacher's mood on entering the classroom, and this seems to reflect on how a lesson may turn out. A teacher that is bright and cheerful can often help students to feel positive and generate a great atmosphere for

the entire lesson, which in turn increases students' ability to learn. If a teacher enters a classroom in a bad mood, this seems to generate negative feelings for the students. And, in most cases, not a lot of learning is achieved and I'm sure a lot of frustration is felt by the teacher.

Only 13 per cent of students said their teacher used a checklist that directly resulted in a grade for results as a way of showing they valued these skills.

Rhonda: 'Checklists' seem to be an excellent form of assessment, but teachers need to inform the students that they are going to use this method—for example: 'Today I am using a check sheet on how well you are able to tutor other students in your table group.' By making this statement, students felt the teacher created a positive method of assessment with all the students knowing exactly what the teacher required.

Although there were mismatches between the outcomes and learning behaviours that teachers actually assess and those that students feel are also highly valued in the classroom, these seemed to be of little real concern to students. Seventy-eight per cent said they would teach English the same way as it had been taught to them (Question 5). The lower figure in Maths (43 per cent) was mainly to do with issues of help (21 per cent), revision (11 per cent) and pace (7 per cent) rather than changes in approach, although 13 per cent suggested more group work. The students did have some specific suggestions, however.

Rhonda: Making a topic more interesting was mentioned several times. For example, in a topic on money (exchanging currencies), students commented that it would be helpful and more interesting if they could actually 'play act' the exchanging of different currencies which would make them understand the procedure better and be more fun.

Students were even less concerned about the way they were formally assessed, with a massive 94 per cent of English students and 70 per cent of Maths students stating they would assess the work in the same way that they had experienced. Maths students did suggest pre- and post-testing (8 per cent) and more assignment work (11 per cent) as alternative methods of assessment.

In interpreting these data, it is important to consider whether or not the students' experiences realistically could lead them to being able to conceive alternatives other than those they had previously experienced. This assertion is supported by data (discussed later) from David's classes that were withdrawn from this sample because he was exposing them to so many different assessment procedures.

STUDENT DATA: CONCLUSIONS

We concluded that, for these students, formal assessment is mainly focused on content, knowledge, skills and comprehension. Given the high numbers of assignments involved, the low rating given to research and presentation was particularly surprising. The students perceived their teachers as formally assessing only a relatively narrow range of outcomes, with other behaviours being acknowledged in less formal ways. This raises questions for us about what students see as valuable. With informal assessments, students acknowledged that teachers highly valued listening, questioning, staying on task and cooperative learning, countering our initial perceptions that perhaps the presentation of work, neatness and good manners would be more highly valued. This is an important point nonetheless, for it illustrates an implicit sense of valuing approaches to learning that might foster understanding. Students did have strong opinions about the assessment they felt was valued in the classroom. It is therefore disappointing that learning behaviours such as questioning, staying on task and cooperative learning were not formally assessed, particularly given the positive reaction from students to the use of checklists (for example) as a form of assessment.

OTHER OUTCOMES WITHIN THE PROJECT

The action research process described in this chapter created a number of other benefits. One was working closely with colleagues and tackling a shared problem. Opportunities for teachers to work closely are rare; meaningful discourse is commonly rushed, with teachers often expressing concerns about their classes and their teaching, but not having the necessary time to discover solutions.

> *Jo*: Initially I was apprehensive about working with David, the Assistant Principal. I was a young, inexperienced teacher whose employment contract was coming to an end and the position I held was to be advertised as a permanent job; David was part of the selection panel. I initially felt that I was 'on parade', with my ideas likely to undergo close scrutiny—something I think contract teachers experience all the time. However, I soon realised the benefits of working closely with someone who was experienced and prepared to listen to my ideas—and offer his own in return. Having time to work on the project with David, Rhonda and Tim allowed us to bounce ideas off each other, to really talk and share our experiences. For that reason alone, the PAVOT experience has been incredibly valuable to my own personal professional development.

> *Tim*: I felt that the process resulted in my own teaching being questioned. I looked critically at everything I did in my own classroom and asked myself the question, 'What would the students say about me and this class?' This self-assessment is absolutely critical if my teaching is to stay fresh and relevant to students. These initial experiences taught me a valuable lesson; constant and constructive reflection on all facets of my teaching is critical if I am to become a good teacher.

> *David*: The project served to reinvigorate/reinforce reflective practice as, although this is always a focus for me, sometimes it becomes masked by the everyday pressures of school. This project became a significant driving force on my teaching over

this period of time. Enduring reflective practice needs support by action research projects like this. I found this action research work fulfilling because of the valuable interaction with the other team members—sharing and, over time, clarifying the problems, ideas and strategies, as well as the excitement I still get in sharing something that really makes a difference. As a group we all became more reflective, the personal growth for all was obvious—as an administrative initiator this is most rewarding and satisfying.

Another interesting outcome of this project was that other teachers noted that having students from their class interviewed meant that they began to look more critically at the content of their lessons and the way they taught. Unfortunately, although it was unintended, the teachers whose students were being interviewed did have a sense of unease, as though their classes were being 'judged'. An interview would not pass without the teacher in question sidling up to the interviewer at recess or lunchtime and asking: 'How did I do?' In one sense, it says a great deal about the staff at this school that they did volunteer to stick their necks out in such a way.

A third benefit was in our own classroom practice.

Jo: I began the project with David after numerous discussions with other staff about the lack of motivation in our Year 9 students. I was teaching a Year 9 Journalism class at the time and we were all struggling to produce a quality school newspaper. Despite giving the students almost complete ownership of the newspaper, they did not seem all that interested in producing quality work or in meeting tight publishing deadlines. After trying various approaches, many of which met with limited success, I was keen to try to address the issue of assessment as a way to tackle their apparent lack of motivation.

I spent a lot of time with the kids changing their focus from work I was basically forcing them to complete to meet the deadline to having them look at the skills and learning behaviours they were developing. I began to publicly acknowledge that these were important to me. I started to assess, with their full knowledge, their interviewing skills, the ways they made links back to previous work we had done in class before coming to me for help and the ways they used each other as a resource. Rather than having my whole emphasis on getting each article produced exactly how I wanted it, with spelling, grammar and punctuation correct, all in a set structure by a definite deadline, I began to encourage the students to produce their articles in a way that suited them. I allowed the students to pair up; those who had trouble spelling and putting their thoughts together were able to dictate what they wanted to say to their partner, who was perhaps more proficient in such skills. Even though the weak student didn't 'write' the article, they still received the credit for it. The students developed a number of articles by using good leading questions and published these, and the answers as they were given, in the newspaper, with students being rewarded for the questions they developed.

We started to use peer assessment, with students doing all the proofing and fixing of errors that I had been responsible for in the past. I gave the students credit for each article they 'fixed'. Even those students who struggled with their skill level were able to participate in this activity as I sat at the computer with them leaning over my shoulder, telling me what they thought sounded wrong or looked wrong, and I fixed the mistakes for them. As a result, I really changed what I was assessing. I started out assessing each student's contribution to the newspaper by assessing the articles that each student had written. I ended up assessing the students on a range of things with the final article produced as the least important. In fact, in the end some students didn't produce any articles, but they did take on roles of proofer or typist or photographer, all of which were equally important. I found that, over time, by equally valuing all of these jobs, the students slipped naturally into where they felt comfortable and work on the paper took off at a great rate.

The finished product was 32 pages of A3 size paper, all typed, complete with photographs, captions and over 100 stories about the school. We had the paper published on proper newsprint and circulated around the town. The final glory was when the students and I received a letter from the local Member of Parliament congratulating them on their fine effort. The next year I had a huge class of students who wanted to produce a newspaper and work started all over again, this time with me being more up-front and open about what I was assessing and what I was valuing in the classroom right from the start.

David: In undertaking this research project, we set out to gather data on the assessment situation 'as it was'. But I quickly found that I began to think more about the purposes of assessment and consequently could not help but develop alternative means of assessment in my own classes. My experience through this research period was one of tremendous professional growth in a very practical way; I continue to develop and use new forms of assessment because of my involvement. In addition to the normal range of tests, assignments and investigations that I would have used, my Maths classes experienced alternatives like peer assessment, checklisting (of learning behaviours, cooperative learning skills, questioning, etc.), oral tests and extended investigations. The following is an example of one assessment experience that I had that was triggered by working in this project.

This example involved the use of oral testing against student-developed criteria (my first in 25 years of teaching)—it was absolutely amazing to see what students really did know/could do compared with a normal written test.

Oral testing in Maths: Pythagoras unit

Students set the criteria:
* communication skills (which they defined further to be clearly explained with written example, eye contact);
* correctness of answer;

- responses to extra questioning;
- complexity of problem chosen to explain.

Classroom management
Students were given a worksheet of 20 application problems of varying difficulty and simply came to me when they felt they had a problem they wished to be assessed on. These assessments were conducted over 2.5 lessons and took 3–5 minutes each to complete.

Observations
- All students were keen to come out for their turn, with some weaker students being the keenest.
- They chose their starting point, with some explaining a problem already written out and, at the other end of the spectrum, doing the most difficult problems from scratch.
- Results were far better than usual with most being 'B result' or better.
- I was able to assist students through troublesome bits by questioning. I was able to clarify what they meant through questioning.
- I was able to further test their understanding by changing their question and by asking additional questions.
- Students were very positive about the experience.
- It gave me the opportunity to discuss with some individuals their Semester 1 progress, with some (significantly) positive improvements in attitude occurring.
- Students appreciated my interest in them as individuals and I felt that some very good relationship development occurred.

As the project progressed, I found myself developing and trying more alternative forms of assessment and having class discussion of assessment issues. This resulted in my class data being withdrawn because it was so different to that from other classes—this all through my impatience, as I wanted to tackle the shortfalls in assessment rather than wait the two years until the project was complete. I felt it was more important to 'get in there' and work on improvements as soon as possible.

As it turned out, these classes generated important data of their own and assisted us with our final conclusions. The discussions, for example, revealed that students can develop clear views on assessment compared with normal classes—who, without such discussion, were 'ignorantly' happy with the way they were being assessed.

A discussion with ten students from David's Maths classes provided some interesting insights:

Only some teachers value other assessments like discussions and structured group work.

Mr Burke liked it when we asked each other questions before we asked him.

Mr Burke would hang over your shoulder and listen a lot.

It is fairer to assess in other ways . . . so that those kids that learn better in other ways can do well.

It helped. It was good to be able to show other skills I had.

It helped me enjoy the subject. I did well. Better than I would have done without it.

I got frustrated when Mr Burke wouldn't help me. But ultimately I did alright so I guess it was OK.

You get to learn skills earlier and put them into practice in the Victorian Certificate of Education [last two years of secondary school]. Sometimes you forget the content but not the skills or the way we learnt.

In David's classes, student involvement in discussions about the project was significant and they liked being involved, with their input valued. It became clear that knowledge can be powerful and that students can make a valuable contribution to the action research process if you take the time to involve them.

> *Rhonda*: I heard some interesting comments from students concerning oral tests, especially students that have some difficulty in expressing themselves with the written word but are able to tell the teacher on a one-on-one basis, without feeling threatened or embarrassed. This method of assessment put students on a level 'playing field', with students that have struggled with other forms of assessment achieving higher grades than previously obtained.

A cautionary point is that it is necessary to broaden one's teaching and learning strategies *before* implementing a broader range of assessment approaches. For example, an extended investigation on measurement, called 'Burke's Backyard' (a popular television show), which was highly successful in promoting independent learning in David's class, was not as successful in some other classes where the Maths teachers (we suspect) tried to teach it rather than allow opportunities for the students to learn it.

PROFESSIONAL DEVELOPMENT: FUTURE IMPLICATIONS

As our experiences demonstrate, research projects lead to outcomes beyond the gathering of data; they are a professional tool in themselves. Some teachers certainly became more aware of trying to assess a wider range of abilities/skills in their classes—checklisting of demonstrated skills in questioning, peer tutoring, on-task behaviour, oral assessments looking at communication skills, ownership/choice and extension to unfamiliar situations were all reported.

The challenge now is to get more teachers to use action research to develop assessment in their classrooms. We recommend employing a

'Rhonda'—an outsider—as a first step in providing the teachers with opportunities for action research in their own classrooms. We believe that this creates opportunities for self-reflection and evaluation, provides teachers with honest and valuable feedback and still guarantees student anonymity. We suggest that the process is enhanced when teachers engage in classroom discussions both about the results they discover and more generally about assessment and what is valued in their classroom.

At our school, where teaching and learning have a very strong focus, we are suggesting the need to meet in either Key Learning Area groups or cross-curricula teaching and learning groups to share ideas about practice and to discuss the implications of different approaches to assessment. In order to allow this to happen, we are also suggesting that the issue of assessment needs to become a school priority and hence attract some resources. Our journey is not over!

REFERENCES

Bloom, B. (ed.) (1956). *Taxonomy of Educational Objectives: The Classification of Educational Objectives.* Handbook 1. Cognitive Domain. New York: David McKay.

Gardner, H. (1983). *Frames of Mind: The Theory of Multiple Intelligences.* New York: Basic Books.

APPENDIX 7.1

1. How did your teacher go about teaching this . . .?

SUBJECT	1. Teacher	2. Groups	3. Discussion	4. Research/ Investigation	5. Activity/w.s.	6. Modelling	7. Other
English	26%	0%	26%	0%	35%	0%	14%
Maths	42%	14%	15%	4%	23%	3%	0%
TOTAL	**34%**	**7%**	**20%**	**2%**	**29%**	**1%**	**7%**

2. What did the assessment task indicate the teacher wanted you to learn?

SUBJECT	1. Content/ knowledge	2. Skills/ how to	3. Interpret'n/ analysis	4. Problem-solving	5. Research	6. Presentation/ communication	7. Links/ communication	8. Comprehension thinking	9. Other
English	1%	32%	40%	0%	4%	0%	0%	11%	12%
Maths	18%	32%	0%	21%	0%	1%	0%	25%	2%
TOTAL	**10%**	**32%**	**20%**	**10%**	**2%**	**1%**	**0%**	**18%**	**7%**

TASK									
Tests	7%	34%	0%	28%	0%	0%	0%	28%	3%
Projects/ assignment	5%	32%	25%	15%	1%	1%	0%	21%	1%
Homework	54%	46%	0%	0%	0%	0%	0%	0%	0%
Other	10%	36%	0%	13%	3%	0%	0%	20%	18%
TOTAL	**19%**	**37%**	**6%**	**14%**	**1%**	**0%**	**0%**	**17%**	**6%**

3. What other skills did your teacher want you to learn?

SUBJECT	1. Listening skills	2. Follow instructions	3. Manners/ quiet	4. Questioning	5. On-task/ work ethic	6. Co-op. learning/ tutoring	7. Presentation/ neat	8. Understanding/ explanation	9. Participation
English	30%	4%	10%	11%	19%	4%	0%	6%	7%
Maths	33%	0%	6%	17%	20%	17%	1%	2%	4%
TOTAL	**32%**	**2%**	**8%**	**14%**	**20%**	**10%**	**1%**	**4%**	**6%**

4. How do you know the teacher values these skills?

SUBJECT	1. Mood varies	2. Uses praise	3. Knows/ tells	4. Uses checklist	5. Other
English	6%	16%	67%	11%	0%
Maths	13%	33%	38%	15%	0%
TOTAL	**10%**	**24%**	**53%**	**13%**	**0%**

5. If you were the teacher, how would you go about teaching this topic?

SUBJECT	1. As it was	2. More group work	3. More enjoyment	4. More help	5. Less sheets	6. Slow down	7. More extensions	8. More revision	9. Other
English	78%	2%	0%	0%	7%	5%	2%	0%	5%
Maths	43%	13%	2%	21%	2%	7%	0%	11%	2%
TOTAL	**61%**	**7%**	**1%**	**11%**	**5%**	**6%**	**1%**	**5%**	**4%**

6. If you were the teacher, how would you go about assessing this topic?

SUBJECT	1. As it was	2. Have pre-/post-tests	3. More assignments	4. Other
English	94%	0%	0%	6%
Maths	70%	8%	11%	11%
TOTAL	**82%**	**4%**	**5%**	**9%**

8

Open Learning: Teaching without a road map

Chris Wilson

Some students have a frustrating habit of greeting the work we prepare for them with the response: 'I don't get it'. Despite our best efforts, it seems to remain our responsibility to teach them. Learning is seen as the passive part of the contract—teaching is the active part that carries all the responsibility. After all, we are the ones who get paid, so it must be our job to do the work.

BACKGROUND

In 1995, I was developing a deep interest in the education of gifted students, partly as a result of my experiences as a teacher and as a parent, and partly through my work over several years in curriculum development in my school. It was clear to me that a significant part of any school program designed to cater for the needs of the higher achieving students would have to be based in the regular classroom, and that it was important to teach these students to be able to work with less dependence on the school system. My reason for thinking this was that the students would inevitably encounter teachers that would be uncertain about how to challenge and extend them, so they would need to learn to do it themselves.

I had observed that many of the students who were high achievers had a close dependence on the teacher to direct their learning, and on the consistent achievement of very good results to maintain a belief in their ability. Far fewer students, in my experience, were truly independent in their learning, and had a good sense of why they were at school, what they needed to get out of their years there, and how they needed to go about achieving these things.

Like many teachers, I had never been comfortable with the notion of a teacher simply feeding information to students, but had developed a belief that students seemed to either have or not have that important but often elusive degree of independence. It was as though it was innate and I was uncertain about whether the teacher was able to make much difference, especially in the confines of a traditional secondary school subject.

PEEL AND INDEPENDENT LEARNING

I introduced myself to Dr George Betts (1992) from the University of Northern Colorado after he had spoken at the International Conference on the Education of Gifted Children in Melbourne. I was impressed by his Autonomous Learner Model (ALM), especially the strong emphasis on the affective domain, and learned that each year during the northern summer he conducted an ALM conference in Colorado. His conference attracted delegates from across the United States and Canada, and took place in a relaxed setting to encourage all participants to share their experiences and expertise in any area related to the development of independence in learning.

I saw independent learning as a critical part of the school program for the more capable students I had been asked to develop, and through my school's Professional Development Fellowship I was able to attend that conference. I was also able to stay on after the conference to spend a week at Dr Betts' Summer Enrichment Camp, where some 700 gifted students, aged from six to eighteen years, from many parts of the United States and Canada, spent an intensive week of activities in many areas of personal interest.

At this time, I was becoming deeply involved in work with PEEL (Project for the Enhancement of Effective Learning) and PAVOT (Perspective and Voice of the Teacher), so I submitted a proposal to present a session at the conference. It was accepted, and in a conversation during the conference Dr Betts asked me how I saw the connection between PEEL and independent learning. I explained that one of the aims of teachers involved in PEEL was to develop more independence in the students—to explore classroom strategies to promote independent learning. He accepted this, but it was not until some time later that I realised it was only part of the answer. The rest of the answer is that, through PEEL, the *teacher* becomes the independent learner, and as such acts as a role model for the students. I have come to see this as one of the most important roles for the teacher in promoting independence in the students.

The PEEL session was very well received. Most of those who attended the session were impressed (or at least intrigued) with the model of teachers learning about classroom learning from and with each other, with little or no direct input or influence from the school itself or the central organising body. In contrast to the way PEEL ran, there seemed to be a much stronger emphasis in the American system on the use of outside 'experts' to deliver professional development, with correspondingly less emphasis on the teachers themselves developing new practices to tackle problems that they had identified.

After the conference, I returned with several initiatives I wanted to implement at my school, and was especially keen to establish a class specifically to promote the development of independent learning. I put a proposal to the curriculum committee, and it was agreed after some discussion that this could be offered as a middle school elective. My Year 12 Psychology class, which was studying 'Learning' at the time, suggested the name 'Open Learning'.

There were sufficient Year 9 and 10 students who chose the elective that a class was able to be run in each semester of the school year. It was neither intended nor promoted as an elective for the high achievers, and the classes were very mixed in terms of abilities and attitude towards school and learning. There were some very capable students who elected to do the subject as a way of developing themselves as learners, possibly with a view to improving their chances of success in the final two years of high school. Others were attracted to the idea of learning through exploring areas of personal interest, while others were placed in the class either to try to salvage their low levels of achievement and/or poor attitudes, or as another class that 'might be interesting' in an otherwise empty block in their programs.

Realising that this would be a learning experience for all concerned, and a fairly uncommon educational venture, I felt it should be the subject of a PAVOT project. I knew that this would be very different from my previous experiences in PEEL; I had had to argue to establish a subject that was not a subject in anyone's experience. The rich pile of wisdom from PEEL about improving learning in established subjects merely told me how much I would have to invent alone and from scratch. Could this be successful? How could we tell whether it had been or had not been successful?

INITIAL THOUGHTS—IN RETROSPECT

Looking at the Open Learning venture with hindsight, I know that I wanted (or hoped) to get to the end of the first year of this subject and be able to say that the students had developed a deeper awareness of the learning process and of their place in it, as well as being able and willing to make insightful comments and observations about their learning.

I imagined teachers coming to me and remarking about how independent, reliable, reflective and aware these students had become; for them to have noticed how their newly acquired learning, organisational and interpersonal skills had been transferred to the other subjects they were studying, and how instrumental these skills had been in improving their grades and confidence.

With the stimulus to hindsight provided by writing this chapter, I realise that a critical gap in my knowledge was the level and kinds of performance in this new subject that would be reasonable for Year 9 students during a single semester. I now realise how crucial this wisdom of experience is to a teacher in reacting to classroom events: what was feasible? possible? probable? high-quality? acceptable? There was no road map available and no alternative but to set out blind, bump into the critical features of this new territory and create an equivalent to a sixteenth-century chart of the Pacific—incomplete but helpful to the next explorer.

OPEN LEARNING THROUGH 1997: AN EVOLUTION

I adapted the original Autonomous Learner Model for use with these classes, because it was originally designed to be used as a progressive development over two or more years. The aim of the model was to take students to a high level of 'passion learning'—a deep learning through exploration of areas of high personal interest—and to have them become more confident and independent in their learning at school (and beyond) through what they had learnt from these experiences.

I arranged and presented the work in three sections during Semester 1:

1. *Personal awareness*: Students would explore and learn about the skills and abilities they already possessed—their strongest intelligences, their learning styles, their level of autonomy in learning, their career aspirations, what they hoped to achieve or gain in their time at school. It was very much an awareness-raising exercise, and also one designed to show that everyone has abilities, not just the capable students.
2. *Skill development*: Students would develop new skills to be used for learning in and beyond school—writing skills, thinking skills, creativity, interview and job applications, research skills, computer skills, goal-setting, time management, audio-visual skills (including gaining their video licences), interpersonal skills. They voted from a lengthy list and the most requested were offered, in some cases using other teachers or the Principal, Student Welfare Coordinator or Careers teacher to run sessions. The students suggested the names of other teachers who they would like to have visit to discuss their 'philosophy of school' with the class.

3. *Research projects*: A series of four projects occupied most of the second half of the semester:

 – Group exploration: In small groups of two to four, the students selected a topic of shared interest and had one week to collect and collate information from as many sources as possible. A report was then presented to the class. This was intentionally a quick research activity designed simply to let the students discover the amount of information 'out there' and readily accessible and available.

 – Individual investigation: Students worked alone to explore a topic of personal interest, and presented a brief report to the class. The use of overheads, charts, computer presentations and video recordings was encouraged.

 – Seminar: Students worked in small groups to prepare and present a seminar to a selected audience. The seminar had to be designed so that the audience *learned* something specific from the presentation. This project involved considerable discussion of what is involved in the process of learning, and how to make the experience effective.

 – In-depth study: This was the major project for the semester. The students worked individually to research and present a detailed report on a subject of deep personal interest—this was meant to be their real passion area. They were required to use multiple sources of information, including a mentor who was an expert in the field if possible, and make a stand-up presentation to the class lasting between ten and fifteen minutes. Planning was detailed, and I spent time with each individual discussing the sequencing of the presentation and how to involve the audience ('Please don't try to just *talk* for ten minutes').

Although I felt that Semester 1 ran fairly well, I was aware that the students were not working at the level I had hoped for. I was perhaps a little idealistic, but in a class designed specifically to develop deeper self-awareness and autonomy I could not be satisfied with conventional teacher–student role-playing—'the teacher gives the work, the students do it, everyone is happy'. It was apparent that, while some of the students were in tune with the aims of the subject, others were not showing any development in terms of taking responsibility for the work. They were turning up twice a week for just another class to do what the teacher told them to do.

I used several reflective sessions in which the students were asked to write comments about the subject—what they had hoped for, how they had felt about it so far, and what they expected to achieve. I even contemplated having the Semester 1 class conduct a small research project on the Semester 2 class, evaluating how well it achieved its aims, thinking that would be an excellent way for them to develop an even deeper awareness of the learning process. But I abandoned the idea as I came to a realisation that they were not taking enough interest in their own learning, let alone someone else's.

A colleague who was interested in the ideas I was trying to develop with this class agreed to conduct some interviews for me about halfway through the semester. This revealed some interesting insights into how the students were feeling. She found, for example:

- A group of three lower-achieving students (selected by me) had little idea what they were trying to achieve, saw the subject as boring and a waste of time, saw little connection between it and other school activities, and felt it was a time to 'talk about what you want to'.

- Three higher-achieving students had a better idea of what we were doing but still had little idea why. They used some attractive terms like 'learning to learn' but could offer little to back up or explain these statements. They saw the class as a comfortable talking time and noted that some of the students did waste time. They commented that we should try more to relate the ideas to other subjects.

As time progressed, these reflective and 'learning about learning' activities and ideas were greeted with increasing resistance:

Not this again!

We've already done this twice.

What do we have to keep doing this for?

I was not sure how to get the students to talk about the subject and how they were feeling about it without asking them directly. I wanted the feedback as a basis for modifying the program, but was meeting increasing resistance. There is little doubt that I was doing most of the learning here.

A significant moment came when one of the more capable, perceptive and articulate students made the observation that the subject 'seems to exist for its own sake'. I asked him what he meant, and he explained (in a round-about sort of way) that he felt they were doing the work so I would be able to ask them about the work they had done, and not because they would gain something more important or long-term from it. Further conversation with him and others revealed that they were finding it difficult to see the relevance of many of the skill development activities we were doing, and were not aware of being able to use these skills in other subjects—or in fact in the projects in this subject. At this stage I was beginning to seriously doubt what I was doing, but knew that it *was* an idea worth persisting with, so I had to make some adjustments to how I was running the course.

SEMESTER 2: A SECOND TRY

I reflected on what I had learnt from this first exploration and made four significant changes from what I had done in Semester 1:

1. I wove the skill development work through the projects rather than treating them as two separate topics.
2. We did the first project, the Group Exploration, in the very first week of the semester. This set the scene by making it clear that the subject was about collecting, processing and presenting information. It was not just about some new skills that do not always 'fit in'. It also created a sense of achievement by completing the first assessment requirement quickly and everyone completed it successfully.

3. I shortened the Personal Awareness section, as it had seemed the least practical or useful, and interspersed the various skill development activities through the remaining projects. This gave the skills more relevance—it was easier for the students to see what they were needed for.
4. I did far fewer reflective exercises, having accepted that I was probably doing them as much for my own analysis of this new venture as for its direct impact on the students' development. I was also feeling a lot more confident now about how this new subject might unfold, so needed less feedback.

The Semester 2 class was similar in structure to the first one:

- It was a relatively small class (about seventeen).
- This elective had been chosen for a variety of reasons—'can choose your own topics to study', 'a friend is doing it', 'will help to learn better at school', 'sounds important', 'parents thought it would be a good idea'—but they had chosen it at the end of 1996, and not mid-year after friends had told them about it in Semester 1.
- It was a true mixed-ability class (mixed in skill levels, awareness, confidence, learning styles, attitudes, feelings about school and learning), and included a few students with moderate learning difficulties (or at least 'learning attitude difficulties').
- There were more girls than boys.
- The students were relatively uncertain about what this subject was and what it was for.

The new structure and sequence worked well. As the semester progressed, we developed a very relaxed and comfortable working environment—we started each double lesson with 'The News' to which anyone could contribute anything current and interesting, we knew each others' idiosyncrasies and made light of them, and we even had a chocolate club, in which we took turns to bring a treat for the group. The much higher level of interest and enthusiasm and the disappearance of the negative comments of Semester 1 were one important source of evidence for me that I was learning how to be a better 'Open Learning teacher'. The second source of evidence was the students' performance. Everyone completed the subject successfully and the diverse and original nature of their final presentations (discussed shortly) reflected students who had taken on board many of the ideas of the course. Their projects were much more exploratory, for example, and reflected higher levels of risk-taking by the students.

I believe that an important factor in this success was that, having lived this totally new experience once, I was more relaxed; I had some sense of a road map with a better understanding of what the students would expect of the subject and me. I increasingly felt as though I had been too intense in Semester 1—trying too hard to make it work and expecting too much.

WHAT DID WE LEARN?

The students

It is not possible to evaluate this learning experience without distinguishing between what the students learned and what I learned.

The pressures of a full-time teaching load prevented me from running a formal interview program and my conclusions are based on the students' performance and attitude and the changes in these areas from Semester 1 to Semester 2. The class included, for example, some whose school careers prior to this had been less than distinguished and who not only developed some new skills and confidence, but also were *aware* that they had done so. These data are supported by conversations with parents who were enthused by the concept of Open Learning and found it a positive and engaging experience for their children, and with school coordinators who found the subject added a new dimension to the curriculum and provided a fresh focus for many students.

I am confident that this was a positive learning experience for all of the students. For each of them it was a class in which the following positives applied:

- They enjoyed *success*. Everyone 'passed', there were many more As and Bs than anything else and I had no difficulty finding positive comments to make on the reports. The students knew beforehand what the nature of those positive comments would be as they were based on the criteria for work that we had frequently discussed as a class.

- They *knew what was required* to be successful. The criteria for each task were clearly spelled out; on some tasks they graded each other's presentations. We talked through how to best meet the criteria and there was never a complaint that they should have received a higher grade than they did—there was never a time when learning was happening without their consent and awareness.
- They developed a greater *awareness of their learning*—we always talked in terms of *learning* as being the thing that school is about; most students seem to see 'work'—the tasks teachers set—as what school is about. We talked about what types of learners we all were. I took part in these activities myself as one active learner in the group. I seldom—if ever—talked in terms of what I had to 'teach' them (because in fact in this subject there *wasn't* much that I brought as an 'expert') and in the seminar they were required to plan and run a learning experience for a selected audience. This turned out to be as diverse as introducing pet mice to preschoolers, helping primary school children learn about orang-utans, helping the class learn sign language and conducting a survey on adolescents' attitudes to the republican movement and Pauline Hanson (an Australian right-wing political figure).
- They developed *new skills*, although the transferability of these remained an issue that was only partly resolved in Semester 2.
- They learned much about *themselves as learners*, including which were their strongest intelligences. We were able to refer to this many times through the semester, always using it to put a positive slant on the abilities they had available to them when thinking about how to approach their school work or plan their potential careers.
- They were treated as *individuals with individual abilities*. There was very little whole-class teaching, as most time was spent on research and development of individual or small-group projects in which they were encouraged to use their individual abilities and newly

developed skills.

- They experienced *diverse ways to collect, process and present their information*. Information was collected from books, computers, experts, videos, and anywhere else they could find. The presentations included survey results on the overhead projector, a video of the preschoolers making mouse masks, comparisons of samples of different songs from a band, an outstanding computer presentation about sumo wrestling, and a video-recorded interview with Dad proudly showing off his Harley Davidson.

- They were able to pursue *areas of interest in depth*. I tried not to be judgmental about the topics selected, and within some guidelines we set as a class they were able to explore areas they would seldom encounter in a regular school curriculum. They may not all have reached Dr Betts' 'passion learning' level, but they were all able to go well beyond their existing levels of knowledge in areas of personal interest.

- They *achieved* things that they would not have thought likely at the beginning, including four oral presentations to the class, two of them on their own. We discussed the importance of going outside our comfort zones in learning, including approaching people for information and making individual presentations to the class or another audience.

- They *enjoyed* the experience, and almost certainly completed the semester with a more positive attitude towards school, what it is for and what it has to offer. One girl even said she was not coming in for the second last week of the year (few Year 9 students do), but would if Open Learning was still on.

The teacher

I began by saying that I knew this would be a learning experience for all concerned, and that certainly proved to be the case. As I finished the semester, I felt very satisfied with what had transpired, and believed there was much to take away from the year. My reflections on my first year of Open Learning can be summarised as follows:

- It *is* possible to teach adolescents about learning. It is a new dimension in teaching that needs time to develop and refine, but it is possible—and we need to learn how to do it in all subjects at all levels. In Open Learning we covered many aspects or dimensions of the learning process, such as skills development, attitude, awareness, and effective and open communication. The students all made progress on all of these, but how much the whole package 'came together' for each of them remains unmeasured.

- Students want to be treated and respected as individuals. The lessons on how to do this that came from Open Learning may not be immediately transferable to other subjects as the activities and skills required will vary, but the principles remain the same. All students are skilled in their own ways, and part of our task as their learning mentors is to show and encourage them how to use their individual skills and abilities. Of particular interest in the Semester 2 class was one boy who needed to be surfing more than he needed to be at school, but learned early in the first term that he had highly developed interpersonal intelligence. That was probably the single most important lesson he learned for the semester, and might well influence his career decision.

  From my position as teacher of this class, it was a rewarding class to be with because the students enjoyed and appreciated being treated in an individual way. It approached what I have always seen as a classroom ideal that is difficult to attain in the regular classroom with the regular curriculum and regular expectations on the part of the students. Open Learning made them think differently about what they were doing, if for no other reason than because it was different.

- We need time, patience and experience to learn how to develop independent learning skills in our students. The approach of requiring students to be so overtly reflective may not be the best one, although this conclusion is drawn from a narrow experience (an elective subject). Certainly it is not the only approach. My experience this year was that, as with all skills we are trying to develop in our students, we need a range of strategies, ways of evaluating whether they are effective and a forum for talking out the many issues that arise.

- It was difficult being the only teacher of this class at this school. English teachers talk about teaching English, PE teachers talk about teaching PE, Grade 3 teachers talk about teaching Grade 3. Who do you talk to in the school about teaching learning? My two avenues were the PEEL groups I was working with, where many of the issues from Open Learning had relevance to what we were all doing in our other classes, and the PAVOT meetings. This experience has made me realise the importance of teachers of all subjects at all levels forming and maintaining professional support networks. I had these networks through PEEL and other groups, but what support is there for the teachers who do not easily form such networks, or have the confidence to seek support? There must be a lot of teachers who do not know where to go for help, but schools do not seem to be very good at providing the opportunity for such networks to develop.

- Students need to feel that what they are doing in any subject is practical and relevant. This need was more apparent in Open Learning because of the lack of conventional content—whether students see algebra or medieval history as important, they at least see it as something they are *expected* to learn at school—and there was certainly an improvement in this aspect of the course in the second semester. As I discussed, the students were tempted to see this subject as not 'real work', yet they continued to do it—usually enthusiastically—when I was able to show them how it was part of their lives. It made me more aware in my teaching in other traditional subjects of the importance of making the work more real to the students, and gave me some new skills for doing this.

- Any experience that requires or encourages us to question our actions is useful. Open Learning was good because, for both the students and for me, it was new, it was different to what we had done before and it had a clear purpose, so it necessitated a lot of purposeful thought. We all learned. There is a scene in the movie *Stand and Deliver* in which the teacher's wife consoles him with 'whether or not they passed the calculus test, they learned'.

POSTSCRIPT

In the two years since I first taught Open Learning, three things of significance have happened:

1. I again taught Open Learning the following year.
2. At the end of my second year of teaching Open Learning, I transferred to a country school.
3. Open Learning no longer exists at my original school: when I invited other staff to learn what I had done and learnt, there was no one willing to invest this sort of effort.

It is apparent now that Open Learning was not sustainable without me there to push it, and this raises what I see as some difficult challenges to teachers, and more so to teacher-researchers. What real value was there in the venture? Am I a better teacher for the experience? Are the students still carrying any benefits from it? Is the school curriculum any less for the loss of this elective? Is what I learnt about Open Learning of any value?

In one important sense it was worth it—most of the 60 or so students who chose Open Learning gained something worthwhile and different from their other school experiences.

As a teacher-researcher though, this experience has made me begin to wonder about the nature of our work and how this differs from the knowledge generation in traditional research. A crucial difference is that the immediate and main recipient of the knowledge and understanding I am able to generate through this research is myself. Developing an early road map and refining it weekly in response to the essential unpredictability of a new classroom initiative was an intensely reflective process. It was risky and messy, but you cannot make a new road map without getting off the road. I enjoy my involvement in this sort of action research because I believe it makes me a better teacher, and my most important work—in my classroom—becomes more rewarding and more enjoyable. This is the reason I have continued with teacher research for several years. It is not possible to know the impact my reports, articles and presentations might have on other teachers and their practice, either directly in their classrooms or indirectly by encouraging them to engage in research, but I know it has made a significant difference to my own practice. It has also redefined how I see the role of teacher.

Given the above, it is less important to me than it might be to more traditional researchers that my assertions and conclusions might not all be able to be supported by substantial amounts of 'clinical data'. It is the very nature of teacher research that we are examining and reporting on our own practice, and that we are more concerned with developing understandings that will have an immediate influence on this practice, and less concerned with conforming to established research protocols. A related issue is that our research is, of course, done within the limited time available, in what is usually a full-time teaching commitment. Having said this, we do want our work to be regarded as credible, in its own way rigorous and useful to others. We are keen to enhance the practice of colleagues through sharing the knowledge we are able to develop.

I am pleased that teacher research recently has begun to gain more status in the area of educational research. Our presentations of teacher research at recent international conferences have drawn (for me) unexpectedly positive responses from both academics and practitioners. I believe that our academic audiences have valued the nature of the knowledge being generated by teacher-researchers and recognised that it is of a different kind—with a much greater emphasis on what is practical and useful as well as what needs to be known to achieve this practical usage. Perhaps it is also communicated in a more accessible format, since effective communication is such a significant part of the teacher's trade. Teachers know what teachers need to know, and teacher-researchers are telling the things that teachers need to know.

REFERENCES

Betts, G.T. (1992). *Autonomous Learner Model for the Gifted and Talented*, Cheltenham, Vic: Hawker Brownlow.

9

The L Files: Motoring towards metacognition in the classroom

Gillian Pinnis

In 1998, I set out to develop a technique that I could use in my Year 7 General Studies class that would teach the students how to learn. I wanted to teach them how to be independent, active learners. I called the technique, or tool, for teaching these strategies 'The L Files'. In this chapter I describe how the program developed and my study of the implementation and effectiveness of 'The L Files'.

INTRODUCTION

Many teachers inadvertently encourage passive learning in their students. Take, for example, the case of the teacher who, at the beginning of the year, handed students a list of 'Rules to Ensure Good Learning'. The list included:

- Get your books ready for learning.
- Be organised.
- Pay attention and listen to the teacher.
- Raise your hand before asking a question.

- Revise your work regularly.
- A quiet environment is necessary for effective learning.

Contrast this list with the types of learning behaviours encouraged in the classroom of PEEL teachers (Baird and Northfield, 1992):

- Plan a general strategy before starting your work.
- Seek reasons for aspects of the work at hand.
- Justify opinions.
- Suggest new activities and alternative procedures for your learning.
- Offer relevant personal examples.
- Seek links between different subjects.

Each of the learning behaviours in the first list is more about classroom management and the promotion of passive learning than active, metacognitive learning. The second, contrasting list encourages the student voice and the development of independence in the classroom.

My aim was to develop a learning environment that encouraged active learning. My first step was to construct criteria that my program would have to meet:

- I required a method to teach students Good Learning Behaviours (henceforth referred to as GLBs).
- I wanted to be able to refer back to the GLBs consistently throughout the year.
- The method needed to be integrated into the curriculum rather than adding to the amount of material that teachers have to teach.
- It needed to be relatively straightforward so that other teachers could use it without undue difficulty.
- Students had to have ownership of their learning and the method to be implemented.
- The method had to be fun.

THE PROGRAM

Using these criteria, I developed a program called the L Files.[1] Each L File was a booklet containing nineteen GLBs. The GLBs were a modified version of a list developed by the first PEEL group. To make the booklets 'cute' and attractive to twelve- and thirteen-year-old girls, they were small and bright yellow. The students had to assemble their own booklets. Each page listed a different GLB and on the back page I added a picture of a car. Appendix 9.1 lists the nineteen GLBs.

To use the book, students had to demonstrate a GLB. When they had done so, they could approach their teacher to sign the appropriate page. When all nineteen pages were signed, the student would be awarded her P Plates and a small red sticker with a 'P' was attached to the car on her booklet to indicate that she was a Proficient Pupil. She would also be awarded a certificate.

Figure 9.1: The first two girls to achieve their P Plates

All Year 7 students (six classes containing over 160 students) at Avila College, a Catholic girls' secondary school, were introduced to the GLBs through this method. Each classroom displayed a poster listing the nineteen GLBs. Teachers of General Studies, a cross-curricula study of Geography, History, English and Social Studies, presented the L Files to the students. At this time, I was the Coordinator of General Studies; hence, in that capacity, I was able to encourage all staff to participate. Incentives were provided occasionally by the staff when interest seemed to wane, or to highlight particular learning behaviours during a lesson or a week. Incentives usually took the form of lollies (candies) or stickers.

The program was not simply limited to General Studies classes. As our school was involved in PEEL, many of the teachers believed that students should be engaged in their learning, and that they needed to be taught how this could be achieved. Staff beyond Year 7 General Studies were also asked to cooperate with this program. That meant that students could, in any class, take out their L Files and request that a page be signed if they had displayed a particular GLB.

I introduced this program primarily to teach students how to become better learners. It soon became apparent to me that it would be worthwhile studying just how effective it was rather than simply trusting my own instincts to gauge the level of success. The study of the program evolved right up to my writing this chapter—which is over twelve months after the first year of its introduction.

STUDYING THE IMPACT OF THE L FILES: DATA COLLECTION

One important source of data has been my own experience as a teacher and the anecdotal responses of my colleagues. Whilst I could not look inside the students' heads to see what they were thinking, I could certainly observe changes in their classroom behaviours. The wealth of informal feedback from both the students and the staff indicated that the program seemed to be working well, but I wanted to check this perception with other data.

As a first step, I added a question to one of my tests that asked students to list as many GLBs as they could remember. The reason for this was to gauge how many GLBs students could recall without prompting. The results are listed in Appendix 9.1. Whilst this was useful in determining whether the L Files were a useful tool for assisting students to remember, or list, GLBs, it was not a means of discovering whether they either understood or used the GLBs. Accordingly, I developed a test on learning, to help determine whether the students really understood what each GLB meant. This test consisted of questions requiring the students to name the GLB demonstrated in each of 38 situations such as the following:

> Kym is stuck. She has to work out the longitude and latitude of a city, but she can't remember which comes first, latitude or longitude. Before asking someone for help, she goes back over her notes to check if the answer is there.

By correctly identifying the GLB that Kym had displayed, the student would have demonstrated that she knew in practice what it meant to use it.

I also wanted to know whether students had taken on board the usefulness of the L Files, so at the end of the year each student was asked to write a response to six questions. The questions were to form the framework of an essay. They were:

1. What are the L Files?
2. What are the advantages of using the L Files?
3. What are the disadvantages of using the L Files?
4. How can the L Files be improved?
5. What are your feelings towards the L Files?
6. How may you use the L Files in the future?

The responses in their essays revealed much more than I had initially anticipated. Students were not limited to reporting in terms of my assumptions (or hopes) as their teacher. There was ample scope for genuine reflection on the whole L Files program and the effect it had had on them. It is worth commenting that, at the time, the students did not see that I was collecting data to study the use of the L Files and so it appeared to them that the need to develop GLBs was simply a 'necessary' part of their education. However, I believe that if students have studied a unit of history and are tested on their knowledge at the end of the unit, then they should similarly be tested on their ability to learn how to learn—the L Files were a part of their learning throughout the unit.

Finally, twelve months after they had used the L Files, sixteen of the original students were asked to complete the following two tasks:

1. List as many GLBs as you can remember (at this stage they had not been given a list of them).
2. Indicate, on a complete list of GLBs, those GLBs you have used in the past twelve months.

The purpose of enlisting the students to assist me at this stage of my study was to determine whether or not there had been any lasting effect from the use of the L Files.

RESULTS

Firstly, I would like to consider how the L Files functioned in my class. This was a particularly inquisitive and lively group of students and most appeared to take part in the program enthusiastically throughout the school year. Some were motivated by a keen sense of competitiveness whilst others sat back and allowed the more dominating students to have their way. At times I found my skills were challenged as I attempted to curb the 'enthusiasm' of particular students so that the quieter students could have their say.

The 'smallness' of the book did attract the eye of the students and it was easy for them to store in their pencil cases. Apart from the fact that several of the books had lost their covers by the end of the year, they were generally quite functional. They valued them and only three were lost. Students referred to them frequently in many classes. Obviously there were times when interest waned and that is when other incentives were used to boost enthusiasm. I have no doubt that my criterion of designing a program that could be integrated into the curriculum without it being too intrusive was met. It was easy for me to be reminded to emphasise the importance of a particular GLB when a student had displayed it or it was an appropriate time to suggest its use. Students would take out their books and leaf through the GLBs searching for the correct GLB, and in the meantime other GLBs were also being reinforced.

Reports from other teachers varied in terms of how much emphasis they gave to the program. Some were enthusiastic PEEL teachers and use of the L Files was easily accommodated into their style of teaching. Some students were frustrated by the fact that other teachers appeared annoyed when they bounded up to them at inappropriate times to have their books signed. I asked my class to establish an agreed-upon procedure between themselves and their teachers regarding times for book signing.

All the teachers of this class reported that there was a high level of engagement in most of the lessons. I observed that an increased number of questions were asked compared with other classes I had previously taught and with other classes I was teaching that were not using the L Files. Students frequently made suggestions about how the lesson could progress or where an activity could be introduced or changed. Classes became flexible forums for discussion and, interestingly, I frequently found myself dispensing with the lesson plan as a result of the direction of these discussions. Students soon learnt that it was OK to admit to not understanding something, or to ask for further clarification—something I viewed as very healthy. The students soon realised that their input was valued.

Getting all nineteen GLBs signed off turned out to be not easy, but seventeen students had more than half by the end of the year. Two students obtained their P Plates, and one started the program again. Both 'P Plate' girls were academically high achievers and rather vocal, confident students. Early on, most of the class appeared to engage in more of the monitoring behaviours of seeking assistance; checking their personal progress; and planning and reflecting on their work. By the end of the year, however, more constructing and reconstructing behaviours were exhibited through students linking their beliefs and experiences, and assuming a position in relation to these.

From a functional point of view, I found the program easy to introduce and incorporate into the curriculum. There was little resistance from either the staff or the students. However, the more important question to be answered is: 'Were GLBs learnt, understood, and incorporated into the students' repertoire of behaviours?'

The results of the 38-item test on learning (explained above) indicated that there was a high level of understanding of what the GLBs meant and that students could identify them. The very high scores indicate that most students had a sound understanding of the meaning of the GLBs and their application in the classroom. Six students scored 100 per cent in this test and only four students scored below 80 per cent. This suggests that, given the context for a GLB in the classroom, students knew what the appropriate behaviour was. The test scores also indicate that the wording of the behaviours was not too difficult for this age group to understand and that they could quite clearly differentiate between them.

The students were given a list of GLBs to draw from to complete the test so I was still uncertain of the extent to which they could, of their own volition, practise these behaviours. I therefore had a question in the back of my mind, 'Do the students need to be able to readily recall the GLBs in order to practise them?' When I asked students to recall as many as they could, there were some GLBs that were listed by almost all the students and others that were only remembered by two students (refer to Appendix 9.1). One outcome of

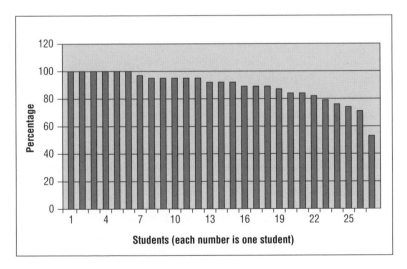

Figure 9.2: Results of tests of students' understanding of the GLBs

the L Files was that students were intrigued by the fact that teachers make mistakes too. Perhaps this is the reason that correcting teachers' errors was the most frequently recalled GLB. It was empowering for them to be able to point out errors—or perceived errors. Often this led to debates about who was correct and why. Frequently further research by the students evolved from the encounter.

The next most frequently recalled GLB, checking of students' work against the instructions provided, was one that led to a dramatic improvement in the quality of the work submitted for assessment. Students could be seen with the instruction sheet beside their completed work, meticulously checking off each completed task and then seeking out the teacher for their L Files to be signed. I would suggest that the frequency of the recalling of this GLB was directly related to their having seen the benefit of this procedure. For me, this was very rewarding.

As Appendix 9.1 shows, when students were asked to recall as many GLBs as they could remember twelve months later, six were not listed by any student. Of note was the fact that the two GLBs just discussed as most frequently recalled at the year's end also featured high on the 'delayed recall' list. The most commonly recalled GLBs were monitoring behaviours. What I regarded as higher order thinking skills tended to not be recalled; however, once prompted by the list, many students said that they had used these.

It is interesting to note that the two students who were first to obtain their P Plates remembered the most GLBs—one thirteen and the other eleven—in the first recall of GLBs. However, another student who only had one page of her L Files signed also remembered 11 GLBs. She, unlike the two girls who had received their P Plates, was a very shy student. This suggests to me that students were learning GLBs but not necessarily being rewarded for the acquisition of this knowledge. I do not think it would be fair to say that she was not demonstrating GLBs, as many times—as is the nature of classrooms—students or teachers were too busy or distracted to take account of the good behaviours occurring in the classroom. Being a quiet student, maybe she was too timid to approach the teacher during a busy lesson to have her book signed.

The two students who received their P Plates scored 95 per cent and 100 per cent respectively on the test of understanding of the meaning of the GLBs. Twelve months later, these students could recall five and four GLBs respectively. Interestingly, though, they each maintained they had practised thirteen GLBs that year. The quieter student, who had previously recalled eleven GLBs, scored 89 per cent on the test. Twelve months later, she recalled four, but maintained that she had practised ten GLBs. She had written in her reflective essay: 'All through secondary school I will refer to the L Files if I don't know what to do. In Year 8 I will use them a lot on everything I do each day. I think lots of people in my grade will be thankful for the L Files when they are in Year 12.' I find her perception of their usefulness very positive; it suggests that the actual awarding of the P Plates was not necessary for all students, as others were content to know and understand what the GLBs were and practise them without reward. However, it was the more confident and vocal students who kept the use of the GLBs on the agenda—something that was important to me as the teacher.

The responses in Appendix 9.2 to the question, 'Will you use the L Files in future?' were very positive, with students variously commenting on the benefits of greater metacognition and improved learning behaviours in their immediate future and in the years to come. Every student indicated their intention to continue using the GLBs or the idea that they would pass the knowledge of the GLBs on to others. Responses such as 'I expect to use these GLBs in the future, in university and in work' were typical. These good intentions were borne out in the responses collected twelve months later. The data in Appendix 9.1 show that all of the GLBs were reported as having been used by at least five of the sixteen students, and thirteen GLBs by half or more of the students. Figure 9.3 displays the number of different GLBs that the students said they had used in the following twelve months. Thirteen of the sixteen respondents said they had practised ten or more GLBs.

I found these results to be most encouraging in light of the original intention of this research—to determine whether the use of the L Files was an effective method for changing students' learning behaviours. Figure 9.3 and the final column in Appendix 9.1 are based

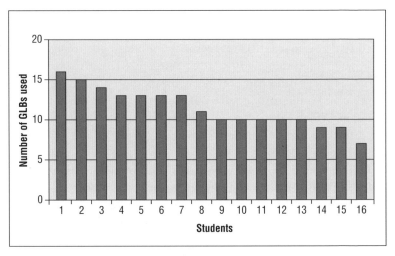

Figure 9.3: Number of GLBs used by students twelve months later

on self-reports and I do not discount the possibility of exaggeration in some student responses; however, there were no prizes and no obvious incentives to purposefully be deceptive.

Once again, behaviours associated with monitoring what they were doing on tasks were reported more frequently than those associated with constructing and reconstructing rich understandings. It may be that the former group is easier for students to acquire, but much more data would be needed before any such conclusion could be drawn.

Overall, the students' perceptions, both at the end of the first year and one year later, supported my rich, front-of-the-class observations that a change in their behaviours had occurred—they had not simply gained knowledge of GLBs.

I believe that, in order for students to change their learning behaviour, they must see advantages for themselves in making those changes. When I asked the students to list what they saw as the advantages of using the L Files, their responses were encouraging. I grouped their responses into four main areas: self-esteem; metacognition; improved performance; and becoming more independent (refer to Tables 9.1–9.4 below).

Table 9.1: Students' perceived advantages of using L Files categorised as self-esteem

If you become a P Plater you should be proud of yourself.

You get the satisfaction of knowing you are a better learner.

Helps me build self-confidence to ask the teacher to sign a strategy.

They give courage to the student for them to be able to communicate and respond to the teachers while they are teaching.

When you get a signature you are proud.

We love to pick up the mistakes of teachers.

The L Files can boost your self-esteem.

Kids aren't afraid to ask for help and feel more confident.

It is encouraging.

Makes you feel good and you know that you have done well.

I feel proud.(Suggested many times.)

I have boosted my confidence and self-esteem. (Listed many times.)

I am confident about my work.

Table 9.2: Students' perceived advantages of using L Files categorised as metacognition

You become aware of your own errors, the teacher's and everybody else's.

It can help you learn from your mistakes.

They help me learn how to learn.

It presents a new perspective.

You think about things before you act.

You are reminded to ask why you got something wrong on your corrected work.

I can see the importance of linking different subjects together.

What surprised me most about the responses in Table 9.1 was the number of times a student mentioned being given courage and increased self-esteem through the program. This suggests to me that having the tools to learn provided students not only with new skills, but also with increased confidence, as they were empowered through the process. The act of pointing out a mistake or perceived error from the teacher is based on the student being aware that their opinions are valued. Other

Table 9.3: Students' perceived advantages of using L Files categorised as improved performance

It can help you learn from your mistakes.

Helps you concentrate on your work.

Helps us fix our mistakes.

They make it easier to understand topics being discussed.

You get to know how the teacher wants you to act and think.

You are learning how to be a good learner and at the same time having fun.

They make learning a whole lot easier and the easier it is to learn the more fun it is.

It helps you improve your work.

You think about things before you act.

You are reminded to ask why you got something wrong on your corrected work.

Improves my learning strategies.

I feel I am understanding more work and discovering new ways to do things.

It encourages you to check your work.

It reminds us how to act in class.

Gives us ideas to brainstorm.

Helps you to study, listen and concentrate.

I can see the importance of linking different subjects together.

GLBs further reinforce the integrity of the student. If students felt good about themselves through this program, one would suggest that they would be more likely to maintain these behaviours (or at least some of them) in the future.

The next grouping of perceived advantages of the program involved metacognition (see Table 9.2).

Whilst the students may not all have known the meaning of the word metacognition, many knew what it was in practice. The responses in Table 9.2 imply both knowledge of thinking about thinking and the value of it. Teachers in other classes also commented on the increased awareness of thinking skills in the classroom. Through the classes' insistence on linking concepts and ideas from one subject (and class) to another, I discovered links I had previously not been aware of. Teachers were able to reinforce learning from one class to another, all motivated by the students themselves.

Table 9.4: Students' perceived advantages of using L Files categorised as students becoming more independent

It encourages you to become more independent.

It can help you learn from your mistakes.

Make you a better learner and make you more responsible.

You can help your teachers learn because we can correct their mistakes.

It helps you improve your work.

Improves my learning strategies.

I can ask the teacher to 're-explain' the work and this helps me.

I particularly like the fact that I can ask the teacher why I was wrong.

It encourages you to check your work.

I have learnt to be more responsible.

Kids aren't afraid to ask for help and feel more confident.

The students also felt that the L Files improved their performance (see Table 9.3).It is obvious from the responses in Table 9.3 that these students have developed an awareness of learning behaviours that goes way beyond the expectations of the teacher (quoted in the introduction to this chapter) who expected passive compliance in the classroom.

Many of their responses also indicate greater independence in behaviour, not just improved performance (see Table 9.4).

Students perceived the application of GLBs as worthwhile. The benefits of taking responsibility for one's own learning are expressed in this group of responses: 'I can ask the teacher why I was wrong', '... makes you more responsible' and 'You think about things before you act'. Each of these implies that the original goal of creating a classroom environment where students are active, independent learners has been achieved, at least for these students.

Finally, one unexpected outcome of this program centred on the role it had in the professional development of other teachers. PEEL can only be a voluntary project and, while our school is considered to be a PEEL school, this does not mean that all teachers are committed to its goals or have a thorough grounding in its practice. Some of these teachers became involved because students were not prepared to demonstrate GLBs in their classes and then not be rewarded with a signature. Students frequently had to argue their case for why they had demonstrated a GLB to a teacher unfamiliar with the whole process and the ideas underpinning it. Of course, there were times when the student had not accurately demonstrated a learning behaviour and discussion followed. Sometimes staff approached me in the staffroom about what a particular behaviour meant and sought clarification for themselves. Both staff and students were therefore engaged in furthering an understanding of GLBs for many in our school community.

In the year that followed, several alterations to the L Files were made in response to students' comments. Several students were disappointed that it took too long to gain their P Plates. To try to alleviate this, the GLBs were divided into two groupings and placed into two separate booklets. The first booklet contained what we considered to be the lower order behaviours and the second the higher order behaviours. The wording was simplified slightly and two GLBs were joined together.

These changes were not successful. Even if some behaviours were higher order, the students did not necessarily progress through the lower order ones first. It was found that students were demonstrating behaviours from the second book when they had not yet graduated to that book. This led to frustration on the part of both teachers and students. At the end of that year, it was decided to revert to the previous idea using a slightly simplified language. Four years on, the program is a well-accepted part of the Year 7 program.

CONCLUSIONS

Our main goal in developing the L Files program was to teach students how to become better learners—to give them the tools to be active, metacognitive thinkers rather than passive students. It is clear to me that, for at least most students, the program successfully achieved this goal.

Collecting and reporting the more formal data reported here was time consuming, but my strong belief that teachers' reflections on their practices are valuable to other educators motivated me to persist. The results have also substantiated my faith in the L Files as a teaching/learning strategy.

Above all, this group of students became very aware of the fact that there is a difference between passive and active learning—that certain learning behaviours would lead them to be metacognitive, to be able to think about their thinking. Students understood the meaning of the different learning practices. Staff, too, have been challenged to allow more reflective and independent behaviours in their classrooms. Professional development occurred without this having been a goal of the program.

The impact this program had in improving students' self-esteem was also significant and encouraging. The skills acquired by them led to their being empowered and in control. The fact that, after twelve months had lapsed, the students' use of good learning behaviours had continued was perhaps the most rewarding outcome of the study. I will implement and further refine the use of the L Files in my classes as I, the teacher, continue to learn how to learn.

NOTES

1. In some states in Australia, learner drivers are identified on the road by attaching a yellow L Plate to the car. After they have obtained their driver's licence, they must display a red P Plate (probationary driver) for their first three years. A real L Plate was attached to all the junior school classroom doors to remind students that they were there to learn how to learn. However, the L Plates proved to be too attractive to the senior students and they soon disappeared.

REFERENCES

Baird, J.R. and Northfield, J.R. (1992). *Learning from the PEEL Experience*. Melbourne: PEEL Publishing.

Appendix 9.1: Data on Good Learning Behaviours

Behaviour	Recall	Delayed recall	Delayed use
I will become a better learner if			
. . . I check the teacher's work for errors and offer corrections.*	22	12	10
. . . I check my work against the instructions which were given for the task, correcting errors and things left out.	18	14	11
. . . I ask the teacher why I was wrong.	16	3	13
. . . I seek links between different subject areas.	14	7	9
. . . I tell the teacher when and what I don't understand.	12	9	14
. . . I suggest new activities and ways of doing things.	9	1	7
. . . I seek links between my school work and personal life.	8	4	8
. . . when stuck, I refer to earlier work before asking the teacher or a friend.	8	3	10
. . . I plan a general strategy before starting.	6	5	12
. . . I seek links between the activities and ideas covered within the topic and from one topic to the next.	5	3	5
. . . I independently seek further information and follow up ideas raised in class.	5	1	7
. . . I offer personal examples which are relevant.	5	1	13
. . . I react and refer to ideas of other students.	5	0	13
. . . I offer ideas, new insights and alternative explanations.	3	0	7
. . . I think about and explain the results.	3	0	10
. . . I know why different aspects of the work are being done.	2	0	6
. . . I check my understanding of the instructions and/or material and ask for further information if needed.	2	2	11

. . . I justify my opinions.	2	0	9
. . . I think ahead and predict what the possible outcomes may be.	2	0	7

Recall = The number of students (n = 28) who remembered each GLB in the end-of-year test.

Delayed recall = The number of students (n = 16) who remembered each GLB twelve months later.

Delayed use = The number of students (n = 16) who reported using each GLB in the twelve months following the L Files program.

* Each statement in an L File began with the words 'I will become a better learner if . . .'

Appendix 9.2: Students' responses to the question: Will you use the L Files in future?

I expect to use these GLBs in the future, in university and in work.

When I need a job.

All through school I'll refer to the GLBs.

If I'm a teacher I will use them in my class.

I'll use them all the time in Year 8.

I'll be thankful for them in Year 12.

I'll refer to them if I don't know what to do.

In the long run they will be good for me.

I'll particularly use 'I will become a better learner if I check my understanding of the material, etc.'

They should be used in all schools.

In future I will refer back to them.

I will remember them right through school and in my job.

I will remember to plan things, check instructions, make links and suggest new ideas in future.

I will think back to it and try to do some of the things that are there.

I will use it as a parent to tell my children or as a teacher to teach my students.

I will always remember the GLBs in future.

I will be more productive in class and be more involved.

I will use them when I get an essay or project.

They will help me with my homework.

They will help me solve problems in the years to come.

If one day I am sitting in class and do get embarrassed to ask for help, I will look back and think that it is good to ask for help.

In future I will check my work against the instructions.

Even if I don't have the files I will still practise the GLBs.

PART 4

Learning through reflective practice

10

Teaching for understanding: The road to enlightenment

Rosemary Dusting

INTRODUCTION

The research described in this chapter is a study of how my practice as a secondary school Mathematics teacher has changed from my early days in the profession. I have examined *where I was, where I got to* and *where I am heading.* Through a discussion of my attempts to develop, employ and critically evaluate an alternative pedagogical style, I have explored how I came to perceive the need for change in my pedagogy; how I came to believe I was a PEEL teacher; and how I examined the implications for my students' learning which resulted from my attempts to be a PEEL teacher. I have investigated how closely my perceptions of my teaching practice matched those of the students I was teaching. In seeking to describe and understand my evolving practice, I hope to illuminate for others something of the interface between what a *teacher* perceives he or she needs to do in order to carry out the rhetoric of *teaching for understanding*, and what the *students* perceive is happening in their classroom.

My PAVOT research was conducted in two stages. The first project was the developmental phase when I had the opportunity to explore and reflect upon new teaching procedures, and the second, several years later, involved an evaluation of my students' perception of my changed practice.

WHERE I WAS

In the beginning

The method I adopted to teach Mathematics was the same as I experienced at school. It worked insomuch as I succeeded in gaining the level of mathematics needed to teach the subject. But then again, I have a certain amount of natural ability, an intrinsic interest in the subject matter and a desire to learn.

Therefore, on my first school appointment, no option for teaching Mathematics had been demonstrated to me other than the traditional exposition model—the teacher in total control of all the knowledge. This was what I aspired to. I actually ignored the strong and abiding memories of the boredom that I had personally experienced in my maths learning at school.

I did not think about the fear of failure I had experienced in my final two years of school mathematics. I suppressed memories about how certain teachers made me feel idiotic if I ventured a response that was incorrect, or how others barely even noticed whether there were any students in the class, rarely leaving their chair or putting down the chalk as they ploughed on through sets of notes they'd been using for the past x years. My teacher training did not illuminate the matter either. When I asked my first Maths coordinator what I had to teach, I was shown the text books, told it was 'all in there' and left to my own devices. There was no advice given as to *how* to impart the content and it was not discussed at meetings. I learned that the teacher closed the classroom door and battled it out alone.

The exposition model

Usually the class begins with an opportunity for students to ask questions about last night's homework followed by writing the topic of the day's class on the chalk board, a page reference, then on to explaining the concept(s). Examples are elucidated—usually graded in terms of their difficulty. During the explanation phase, the teacher stands at the front of the room, facing the class, monitoring responses and behaviour. Usually students are asked if they 'understand', or if there are any questions. All responses, with hands raised, go through the teacher. Students are quizzed by cloze or recall questions with a one-second wait-time. Then a set of similar problems are set for the students to work through individually. The class may work quietly or silence may be insisted upon. The teacher may move around amongst the students, assisting those who are stuck, or may catch up on corrections at the front desk.

After sufficient time has elapsed, some further problems to practise the algorithm will be set. Students know what to expect: it is predictable and stable. The exposition to a group of people simultaneously is very time-efficient—preparation time is minimised, which is important for busy, overworked teachers. Confident students have the chance to display their ability whilst quiet students have the opportunity to seek assistance one to one as the teacher moves around the room.

The need for change

Initially I tried to perfect the exposition style and to develop a repertoire of methods to keep students quiet whilst I told them what they needed to know. Thus the type of questions I asked myself (see Table 10.1) about the quality of my teaching and my students' learning tended to be restricted to blaming myself—or the students—for any perceived lack of success. I had a sense of responsibility for *making* students understand and remember. It was *my* problem. I had to show them what to do. If I did not show them properly, then they would not learn and I would have failed.

An event in my first or second year of teaching was a catalyst for change. A Year 9 girl wrote a page of suggestions about how I could improve Maths classes and handed it up with some homework. I was deeply offended! How would a student know what problems a teacher

Table 10.1: Reflective questions I asked myself about teaching/learning

- Have I really taught some of these students anything?
- What must I do to explain things better?
- Why don't they seem interested sometimes?
- How do I deal with 'stupid' questions?
- Why don't these kids listen: they just aren't trying!
- I TOLD them how to do that!

faced? I chose to ignore her remarks—I can still picture her face as she collected her work looking for my response. I saw she was firstly expectant, then crushed, then disgusted. Deep down I was ashamed: part of me knew it had been perfectly legitimate for her to offer her comments—she had taken a considerable risk. Sadly, she did not bother again. She just bided her time until the year ended. I felt threatened and had not wanted to formally recognise this student's voice—the agenda was about me and my teaching. I did not realise until much later that this was a rare student. Most students do not want to be taught for understanding—or see the need for it. She helped me begin what has become a continuous process of reflection upon, and change in, my practice.

I came to realise that some of the problems I had been having helping students learn Maths for understanding were due to two factors: the inherent weaknesses of the chalk and talk transmissive model; and the fact that it was the only style I was using.

Student interest and engagement were not so easily aroused, and behaviour and classroom management problems arose as students became bored and disaffected. Some students did not understand the work and turned off, feeling like failures because they did not 'get it'. Students had little chance to experience and practise thinking skills. Students' questions were channelled through the teacher who decided what was relevant to discuss. I had no clear ideas about how to help students become independent learners and I was only vaguely aware of the ideas of metacognition, constructivism and quality learning.

WHERE I GOT TO

Implementing the changes

In 1994 I embraced the ideas of PEEL (Baird and Mitchell, 1986; Baird and Northfield, 1992) because I wanted to change my practice. The theoretical base and generic teaching procedures were the perfect vehicles for risk-taking and growth. I became involved in my first PAVOT project in 1995. During this year, I worked with a group of six like-minded teachers as we trialled new teaching procedures. We discussed them, evaluated them and wrote about them, a process which culminated in the publication of a book (Dusting et al., 1996). PAVOT facilitated a significant shift in the nature of my teaching. I hoped I was becoming a PEEL teacher, because I was doing PEEL things.

The next phase

By 1998, I was attempting to more consistently teach for understanding. I tried to base my teaching on aspects of the Twelve Principles of Teaching for Quality Learning (Mitchell and Mitchell, 1997). I began to ask myself reflective questions (see Table 10.2)—note the contrast with those in Table 10.1. Metacognition became important and deepened my understanding of my teaching.

Table 10.2: Reflective questions as a result of PEEL involvement

- Did we make any links between the ideas in this lesson and those taught in the last one?
- Did I provide an opportunity in this lesson for the students to work out some of the content for themselves?
- Is the understanding students have of the content a result of their having constructed their own personal meaning, or is it more superficial, based on processes rather than the reasons for the processes?
- Have I helped the students in this class learn how to learn?

- Do they understand how they, as learners, best learn?
- Can they distinguish between a good question and a functional question?
- Can they make their own notes, construct accurate meanings and monitor their own progress?
- Do they realise that the teacher does not have to 'tell' them in order for learning to occur?
- Can they move independently from 'confusion' to 'clarity' without needing to be bailed out every time?

ACCELERATING THE CHANGE

That year, 1998, turned out to be my year of greatest change. I attempted to continue to incorporate the best aspects of the formal traditional method and to make regular use of PEEL procedures. Most importantly, I was trying to come to a better understanding of what it meant to be a PEEL teacher.

Increased risk-taking

Occasionally, instead of writing formulae on the board and demonstrating how to apply them, I challenged my students' passivity by writing only the heading on the board and asking them to find out for themselves the information in their textbooks that was appropriate. I began to ask the students to read attentively, to memorise a new rule or procedure, because two students would be randomly chosen to come and write the information on the board and offer a brief explanation. I publicly acknowledged the students' risk-taking and there were very few negative comments from other students about 'mathematical errors'. In fact, the other students watched intently as they checked to see the information. Following some discussion, students would then assess the exercises in their texts and nominate, with reasons, the particular exercises they, as a class, now had enough knowledge to complete. Students were sometimes invited to choose how many questions of a certain type they personally needed to complete to be satisfied that they could do the work.

As I watched students learning this way, I genuinely felt that I had created circumstances in which there was engagement with the task, concentration, active student involvement, risk-taking and increased interest. My teaching had shifted from me doing all the work *for* the students to the students now working out part of the content for themselves. They had been provided with meaningful opportunities to think and I had not taught by *telling*. This felt to me like good PEEL teaching.

Working from the knowledge base of my class

I came to recognise that many students viewed lessons as separate, isolated events. I therefore developed a variety of ways of tapping into students' prior knowledge to improve their *linking*. At the beginning of a new topic (e.g. measurement, probability or statistics), I began to use *brainstorming*. This became an effective way of collecting and considering many of the relevant words/phrases that students knew about the topic. When using this technique, I tried to ensure that everyone made a contribution. Some excellent teaching possibilities then opened up:

- The words could be written up according to a predetermined organising principle that the students had to deduce, then I could ask them to work out appropriate sub-headings to further organise the principle.
- The information could be compiled into a set of notes by individuals or groups.
- A concept map could be constructed from the information.

In providing opportunities for this type of activity, I felt I was demonstrating that their prior learning was clearly valued. Also, students would see that what they had previously learnt was useful. I believed that if they were personally involved in these processes, they would own the information. Consequently, we were also able to discuss how, during their learning, they processed information—not typical in a Maths classroom.

Giving students the opportunity to write their own notes

Sometimes, after class discussions or other activities, students would be invited to write down their understanding of a concept. For example, I asked them to construct their own definitions; identify the steps in using an algorithm; or write in their own words the steps used to solve a problem. A powerful insight emerged for me through this process. Once the students were familiar with the expectations of these approaches, they (generally) became quite accepting of the tasks. They quickly got down to the process which involved writing; they listened attentively as others read out their versions; and they checked and altered their own writing as a result of what they heard and now thought.

My understanding of what it meant to teach students to be active learners was being developed and I valued what was happening:

- I found that students were engaged and attentive when they knew they constructed their own notes.
- There was little down-time spent in copying notes off the board.
- I anticipated that through this process students would come to appreciate that recording notes from the board (or their textbook) is of limited value if they have not been involved in personally processing and constructing meaning—this is certainly a challenge considering what students' existing ideas of school learning entail (Loughran and Northfield, 1996).
- I hoped that, by providing opportunities to value students' thinking and telling them so, they would come to understand more about metacognition.
- I thought that I was helping students to see what it meant to be independent learners and to take some responsibility for working out the content for themselves.
- I felt that, by listening to other students' explanations, they were experiencing different ways of expressing the same information and that their own understanding would therefore be enhanced.
- Different learning styles were being used when students listened, interpreted and then translated the information into text.

All in all, I believed that, considering what I had experienced in Maths classes in the past, much richer learning experiences were being provided in this classroom environment.

Asking higher order questions

Another shift in my mindset was to think about and improve the quality of the questions I asked my students. This was a difficult area in which to achieve change because the day-to-day business of managing a classroom sometimes overwhelmed my best intentions. Despite my growing appreciation of what constituted excellent questions, I sometimes forget to ask them, or else they occurred to me after the event.

I have come to see that the first aspect of questioning involves stimulating students' thinking by *asking* them good questions. I have a vague memory that at some time I was once told that research suggests that 80 per cent of teachers' questioning is at the memory/recall level—minimising processing skills. I now understand what that means and what a shift in questioning entails. For example, I tried asking questions that were not the normal convergent, closed Maths-type questions. I shifted to questions like those in Table 10.3, as I thought they fostered better thinking.

Table 10.3: Thinking questions

- Are both these situations examples of the principle?
- Tell me two similarities between these questions.
- Can you justify your reasoning to the others?
- Can you provide me with a counter-example?

I came to see the importance of 'training' students to understand what a 'good question' was. When a student asked a question such as, 'What if . . . ?' or 'Does that always work?' or 'But didn't you say that . . . ?' or 'Is Question 4 an example of that as well?', I would draw attention to it for both the individual and the class as a whole—I was specifically trying to build my students' metacognitive powers by noting examples of quality questions as they were asked.

Another interesting shift was that I did not always answer a good question, but instead often deflected it to other students with responses such as 'What do other people think about that?' This was to show that I valued their views and that I was not the sole arbiter of right or wrong. This created other opportunities, as I could respond with 'I was thinking about that too' or 'See what I can come up with tonight—you can all think about that too'. This approach was designed to convey the message that I am not always certain of everything, and that it is acceptable and realistic to *not* know everything immediately.

Using longer wait-time

A further significant change to my practice was to model longer wait-time when students asked questions. I let students know that I was paying attention to my wait-time in both whole-class and one-on-one situations. I explained that this meant that I did not expect answers to be 'blurted out' before everyone had had time to think. It was gratifying when students began to patiently wait for others to respond—although this took constant reinforcement. It was satisfying to be able to thank students for their contribution after they had successfully thought through the answer to a question. This became another opportunity to not only raise students' belief in their ability to work things out, but to provide them with the *chance* to work things out. Occasionally I found that I had had formed a view of a student's ability that was drastically altered when I gave her time to demonstrate the reasoning that underpinned her statements/answers.

I have a strong image of one lesson in particular when a girl was working out the answer to a problem on the chalkboard. She was stuck, but was determined to complete the task. The rest of the class simply waited for her to get 'unstuck'. 'Look, you can see her thinking, can't you?' a girl near me whispered. They gave her quite a few minutes, waiting quietly, and the breakthrough came when the student completed the question and the class rewarded her with 'Yeah, I got that too!' and 'I agree, yes, I think that's right.' She sat down beaming. Incidents such as this illustrated for me that my practice was beginning to fulfil my teaching aims and that students had begun to blossom as independent learners.

Promoting and using student talk

I constantly tried to reinforce the idea that, by demonstrating and explaining their reasoning, students would be provided with a very important way of homing in on misconceptions. I especially welcomed students who *volunteered* to show both me and the rest of the class their different ways of obtaining solutions. Some of the best moments were in questions like 'Can I come out and show you?' followed by taking the chalk and proceeding to demonstrate a point. One day, two Year 9 students wrote on the board their answer to a certain algebra question. I was secretly ecstatic when two girls approached me and requested that they write up their solution step by step next to that of the original girls': 'We know we mightn't be right, but our answer is different and if we compare their steps with ours we can work out what is happening.' This is exactly what occurred, and everyone watched with great interest. The initial solution was correct and the second pair worked out where they were going wrong. The rest of the class had the opportunity to see the different working out and therefore better understand the situation and the thinking that underpinned the maths being completed.

I also encouraged students to assist others (and to better develop their understanding) by allowing them to move around the room and ask for help. Sometimes several students started to explain ideas across the room to others during whole-class discussion. When this situation took off, it was very exciting. My perception was that students were valuing their own thinking and had confidence in their ability to express themselves. Creating the conditions that allowed students to teach each other required a willingness to take risks and to relinquish the power of being *the* transmitter of the knowledge—along with a recognition that I was not necessarily the one who knew how to best explain the work to everyone.

Students who are 'stuck'

Like most Maths teachers, I tire of phrases such as 'I don't get it'. My 1998 students learned that they needed to be able to identify exactly which part of a procedure or algorithm they were stuck on and frame a useful question that identified the parts they did not understand, before I would assist them. I wanted them to understand that they should share the responsibility for their learning and I tried to make this explicit for them through modelling the language of learning: 'It's important that you think about that and make the link for yourself, you will remember it better in the long run.'

If, when I returned to a student, they said 'Don't worry, I've worked it out now', I considered that I had allowed them to learn. I tried hard not to resort to just telling. I asked students whether they had checked other resources first. They began referring to their notes, looking for similar examples and engaging in discussions with other students. If a student remained stuck, then I encouraged them to re-read the question to me and to underline the key words. If I needed to explicitly explain a set of procedures, then I asked the student to paraphrase what I had said and to repeat it back to me.

WHERE I AM HEADED

Feedback from students

Towards the end of 1998, I was fairly sure I was doing quite well as a teacher who was purposefully encouraging students to be active, responsible learners. I was also beginning to better understand what teaching for meaningful learning really meant. My teaching had progressed in ways that I found much more professionally satisfying. I knew I could never go back to where I had started. However, I was still uncertain whether my teaching was actually resulting in better quality *learning* for my students. I felt a need to determine whether or not the students genuinely understood the purpose in my teaching— what were their views about the way they had been taught? I wanted to know how my teaching had impacted on their learning. Had the students developed an appreciation of some different and independent ways of learning? Were they learning to work more effectively? An important aspect of my personal understanding of what it truly meant to teach for understanding, to enhance students' metacognition and to develop an active learning environment was to determine whether the students could discern and appreciate any differences between my teaching style and that of other teachers.

For these reasons, towards the end of 1999 I conducted a survey of the entire Year 10 level. In this way, I hoped to obtain data from two classes of students who had been in my intensively 'PEELed' classes in 1998. I was concerned that asking students to remember Maths classes twelve months after completing Year 9 could be problematic. I also surveyed my 1999 Year 9 class because I wanted to compare what turned out to be a less intensely 'PEEL' year with the previous one.

All 118 Year 10 students in the sample were given the survey to complete simultaneously and anonymously. In order to analyse the data, I grouped the two classes I had taught as Group 1 (42 students) and all other classes as Group 2 (76 students). My 1999 class became Group 3 (25 students). Groups 1 and 2's responses to the invitation to 'comment on the teaching and learning style you experienced in Year 9 Maths in 1998' were interesting.

The first significant observation was that the students from both groups definitely recalled the teaching style from twelve months before. I was surprised by the clarity of their responses. Of those in Group 1, some recognised a difference and were quite positive about it:

We learned through a number of different methods which did assist us.

I believe it was effective for many different ways of learning and memorising were experienced.

The learning style was OK. We learnt to work independently because there were no explanations—the answers were from questions. It has probably benefited us as a result.

I learnt quite a lot—it was full on.

We were taught to think for ourselves. I learned how to work in groups in problem-solving.

It was really good—I enjoyed it.

Other classmates found it difficult, however it was all right for me.

I guess . . . I learned using examples in the textbook. I also learned with my classmates, which helped me understand the topics more easily. The learning style helped me to work independently . . . when I don't understand anything then I'd rather ask a friend or figure it out myself from the examples in the textbook.

It was good in a way—preparing us for Year 10 Maths.

She taught us well.

I found that I learned by interpreting things for myself and changing the language used to help out fellow students that didn't understand. Also by asking others and discussing.

This group of comments is encouraging because it indicates that these students were clearly aware of my attempts to help them learn differently. There is implicit evidence that their learning was of a different (and higher) quality. These students' responses illustrate that they appear to have appreciated the opportunities provided for them to monitor their own understanding.

Four students did not seem to notice anything different:

The teaching style was OK where most things were done on the board. I learned a lot in Maths last year.

Pretty much just listen and learn and keep up with all your work. If you did that you were fine.

I thought that our teacher moved very quickly without giving us the time to think for ourselves or to ask questions.

Same as every other year but more group work and games.

Other students perceived the difference, but had some reservations:

Often I needed to teach myself things. It was good in a way but at the time really confusing.

It was all right and taught you to work independently but I often hated having to teach myself as I often became confused.

This was a 'Do it yourself' atmosphere . . . if I asked questions I was made to feel dumb. This year I have been taught by a very structured teacher and my marks have improved considerably. I guess learn it by yourself benefits some but it did not benefit me.

I didn't find the teaching style to be very successful but some people found it to be very good . . . there wasn't enough explanation or examples. I was encouraged to learn a lot on my own with little help from the teacher which is good sometimes but not all the time.

Asking other students for help other than the teacher was good but it also interrupted others while working.

Overall good but not enough time was taken to explain to those not understanding.

It was good but at times things were not explained clearly enough.

Still others perceived a difference but expressed some negative feelings about their experiences:

I had trouble processing and understanding some things because my teacher didn't explain things well.

The teaching style was not good. I would go to other students for help.

We were expected to do things on our own with no real explanation.

It was poor. I was taught by other students not the teacher. Other students used their time to teach each other because the teacher was not doing her job properly.

I practically taught myself. My teacher wasn't very helpful when it came to questions I didn't understand.

A year with little help or encouragement and spent most of the year trying to work things out by myself. It was a harder year than this [year] because it took longer to work things out.

I had to teach myself some things or get my family to help me because it wasn't explained in class.

Considering what I was trying to do, and despite the students' frustrations, there is an apparent mismatch between the way in which some students perceived what was happening and what I was observing and valuing. I had at times been quite delighted when students had worked out answers by themselves or had demonstrated other good learning behaviours, but for some students these occurrences may not have represented the success for them as learners that I had perceived it to be as their teacher. Further, some practices that I had actively fostered, such as setting up the classroom environment so that students could improve and reinforce their own learning by teaching a new idea to someone else, were viewed negatively by a number of students—to the extent that one student thought that the students had to explain the work to each other because I had not been 'doing my job'.

Although I thought I had consistently tried to use a language of metacognition and to clarify why I was teaching in the ways outlined above, in some cases I obviously did not overcome the deeply ingrained expectations that some students have of their Maths teachers. Telling them why I was teaching in this way did not convince all of them that it was a better way. Northfield (Loughran and Northfield, 1996) encountered similar resistance in his teaching, which he interpreted in terms of the years of experience students have with the stereotypical model of school teaching and learning. He reasoned that students grew to expect to be taught in a teacher-directed way and learn not to think too much for themselves—it is both difficult and tiring.

I have come to see that these expectations of the way Maths teachers 'should' operate are strongly reinforced by parents, whose indicative comments at parent–teacher interviews reinforce students' understanding of what teaching and learning is meant to be:

> I always tell her, if you don't understand something then *ask* the teacher. That's what she is there for—to *explain* it to you.

My experiences through the examination of my teaching and my students' learning now makes statements like this to be much more revealing than I may have once realised. The implicit message is that the teacher does the learning for the students—that is the teacher's responsibility.

It took a great deal of energy and conviction to sustain the alternative teaching style I began to develop in 1998. It would have been easier to just tell. My data supports Loughran and Northfield's (1996) findings, which make it plain that there is resistance from the 'guardians' of 'correct practice' if school teaching and learning is to be more active, responsible and purposeful. I am sure I challenged many students to move out of their comfort zone and that quite a number did not like that challenge. However, I do not believe that such a view, in itself, is sufficient to neglect the need to teach for understanding.

Student responses from Group 2 (students from other Maths classes) provide further evidence that the traditional model is highly valued by many students. There was considerable diversity in the

Group 2 comments (they had four different teachers), yet a number offered a view similar to the following:

> The teaching style was very good because the teacher explained everything thoroughly and if we needed any help the teacher would be happy to explain it.

> The teaching style was great. Things were explained fully or until understood by the whole class. We did examples together on the board and then we completed our exercises.

> It was very good because the teacher made us all feel comfortable about what we had to do. She answered all our questions.

> We were given examples on the topic and everything was explained to us so we would understand. Then we would do set exercises.

Significantly, there were very few comments of this type about *my* teaching from the students in Group 1. I would have found this devastating at the beginning of my teaching career, but I now interpret this data as strong evidence that my different teaching approach was recognised—if not always appreciated.

Loughran and Northfield (1996) have indicated that many students do not distinguish between being able to do the work and understanding the work. Students in my class were often asked to try to truly understand the work. This inevitably led to learning demands that could well be perceived by many students as unnecessary; further, they believed these extra learning demands may go unrewarded in conventional assessments such as written tests.

These concerns were also raised in my mind. Despite my best intentions, some of my students felt as though I had not been drawing the threads together sufficiently well for them:

> It would have been really good to teach yourself and then have the work re-taught by the teacher so you had a really clear idea of what you were doing.

I certainly recognise that, in teaching, it is not sufficient to 'throw' out some ideas, wait, then allow time for discussion and exploration if the overall big picture, the purpose underpinning the approach, is not made clear. It seems to me that I had not done this well enough for some of my students. I personally found it very challenging to 'draw the threads together' when students had come to their understandings via different routes. The difficulty in validating different means of thinking and explaining without prescribing the method is a big ask for a teacher.

A telling response from a Group 2 student was:

> She would write out the steps and go through it with the class and leave time for questions. It is the teacher's method of teaching that puts impact [sic] on students' learning. It is only when you understand something that you like it.

Inadvertently creating feelings of confusion, and not resolving them, can be disastrous. Learning needs to be carefully monitored to avoid a greater risk of such confusion and lack of resolution occurring when pursuing teaching and learning in the way that I have described through this chapter. My uneasy feelings about this issue have been verified by my research. I have learnt that I need to use my professional knowledge to respond to contextual factors and to step in and clarify when I see the need.

Further modifying my teaching

At the beginning of the 1999 school year, I surveyed my 25 Year 11 students about 'What makes a good Maths teacher'. The majority wrote 'explains things', 'goes slowly' and 'gives good examples', and the general tenor of their comments was very conservative. This, together with my concerns about whether my teaching in 1998 had resulted in improved learning, combined to make me tone down my approach. Another pressure I felt was the need to cover sufficient content so that my classes would 'measure up' in common assessments. The paradox for me is that I know that slowing down and allowing more time for students to construct their understanding makes for better learning and that students therefore do better on *those* sections of a written pen/paper test. However, they do worse overall if they simply do not 'recognise' some of the questions on common assessments because they have not been exposed to the content due to lack of time.

I therefore became quite curious about my 1999 students' views of my teaching and how they compared with the 1998 cohort. These are the Group 3 responses to the same stimulus question that the 1998 cohort responded to:

> It was really open. The teacher really made you work things out and didn't explain everything on the board. Everyone helped everyone else pick up concepts and ideas so it was a really good working environment.

> The teacher gave us a chance to use previous maths skills and expand on them. It was good because we didn't always work out of the textbook.

> The teaching was usually very well explained and after each new concept was taught I understood it. I liked it when I, or anyone else in the class, wasn't sure of something the teacher would slow down and try to make it clearer . . . I was encouraged to think for myself and be an independent learner which I think is very good. I also felt that I was challenged. I enjoyed this class a lot.

> I like the style better this year because it was more varied. It wasn't always sit down, take notes and do exercises.

> The teaching style was more intricate. Very different to that of previous years.

> The class was like a forum where everyone was equal. Studying and listening are the key, and asking for help.

Maths has been fun this year ... because we all feel comfortable to ask questions.

We had to teach ourselves rather than learning at school. But it is a good experience for us because when we get to Year 12 [final year of secondary school] we'll need to study for ourselves.

It was different to that of my last teacher so it took a while to adjust but I got there. I liked the independence we were given. I enjoyed Maths this year due to the independence and freedom and the range of styles in which we were taught.

It was good. It took a little while to adjust to but I eventually enjoyed it. Very different to previous years because we had more freedom but it was very effective.

My learning speed has increased and I still understand.

It was very different: fast, enthusiastic and original.

Not all viewed the teaching and learning this way, however—some students saw it differently:

Most of the time the teacher would explain then we would do examples as a class. We would then do exercises from the book. I learnt well but at times it was boring.

The teacher spent half a lesson explaining what we were learning about and people asked questions. The class was involved in working out problems together. Then we spent the rest of most lessons working out stuff from our textbooks. I learned a lot.

It was OK. Sometimes I didn't quite get stuff but my friends would help out. Sometimes the teacher rushed subjects. It was a good learning style, sometimes confusing, but good.

So again my students recognised a difference. This year I was deliberately more balanced in my approach. I became more adept at finding appropriate responses to my students' needs. Most of these students were comfortable but still felt challenged. They acknowledged that they had been taught differently, and were aware of the purpose for that difference. This group was learning in ways congruent with the aims of my teaching but I was less concerned with watching myself *teach* than with watching the students *learn* in better ways.

CONCLUSION

Realistically, in time, I expect my students will have forgotten details of *what* they were taught but I hope they retain a real understanding, and a genuine knowledge, of *how* learning can best occur. I believe my research suggests that this is possible. Most of my students experienced a variety of ways of learning, and understood that there was an expectation placed upon them to be active participants in their own learning.

As a result of my PAVOT experience, I now have constructs and a language available to me to reflect upon and develop my practice. My mindset has changed. I am now aware of being able to abstract from one situation to another and to recognise and further develop a generalised knowledge about my own practice.

Although it is difficult, I have found that it is possible to create a classroom environment whereby my ideals are increasingly achievable aims, not just rhetoric. There will always be a difference in the perceptions and expectations of students and teachers about teaching and learning, and this will always present challenges—it is the nature of the complex world of teachers and learners. However, I now believe that I can honestly claim to have a better sense of how to shape my students' expectations of how to become better learners.

Through this research into my teaching and my students' learning, I have been reminded about how important it is to not only attend to my agenda as the teacher, but to focus similar attention on the students' agenda as well.

REFERENCES

Baird, J.R. and Mitchell, I.J. (1986). *Improving the Quality of Teaching and Learning: An Australian Case Study—The PEEL Project.* Melbourne: PEEL Publishing.

Baird, J.R. and Northfield, J.R. (1992). *Learning from the PEEL Experience.* Melbourne: PEEL Publishing.

Dusting, R., Pinnis, G., Rivers, R. and Sullivan, V. (1996). *Towards a Thinking Classroom: A Study of PEEL Teaching.* Melbourne: PEEL Publishing.

Loughran, J.J. and Northfield, J.R. (1996). *Opening the Classroom Door: Teacher, Researcher, Learner.* London: Falmer Press.

Mitchell, I. and Mitchell, J. (eds) (1997). *Stories of Reflective Teaching: A Book of PEEL Cases.* Melbourne: PEEL Publishing.

11

Changes that matter

Amanda Berry and Philippa Milroy

Let it be known that there were two of us . . . We put ourselves forward as a teaching team. It was an unusual work situation and it seemed to give us permission to do things in unusual ways. It was the opportunity to try together to put consistently into practice the ideas we shared about teaching and learning.

INTRODUCTION

We are two Science teachers who shared the teaching of our middle school Science classes over a two-year period. This chapter describes some of what we learnt about our teaching, our students' learning and ourselves as we attempted to put our beliefs into practice by exploring the question: 'What are the aspects of our practice that we need to develop and/or change in order to teach consistently and effectively to address our aims?'

Our aims were to:
• teach in ways that would facilitate students' better understanding of science concepts;

- foster students' responsibility for their own learning; and,
- work from the position that science is a social process and that science ideas change over time.

We will specifically trace one of the threads—teaching for conceptual understanding—which we see as an important teaching goal. Our observation of students' Science learning illustrates that many students have fragmented collections of Science facts that are mainly applicable in tests, but are unconnected to other topics/subjects or their lives outside the classroom. Therefore, helping students understand Science concepts as something other than isolated facts means that they might construct a more meaningful and connected knowledge of Science.

In recounting our shared teaching experience in this chapter, we present a series of snapshots from our classes (drawn from journals,[1] curriculum documents, our memories of conversations, and students' recollections of our approach and their responses to it), in order to illustrate different elements of our approach and the particular challenges associated with putting our beliefs into practice.

ATOMIC THEORY AS OUR CONTENT VEHICLE

While most students are likely to encounter atoms in their Science classes, many find the ideas challenging, and the learning of chemistry tends to become reduced to descriptions and procedures rather than any meaningful understanding of the concepts and their applications.

A BIG COMFORTABLE LIE . . .

Snapshot 1: Exposing the assumptions

The school's curriculum document outlined our teaching brief: to go through the structure of the atom and quickly move on to work with ions, molecules and simple chemical reactions. We felt uneasy about this as we had been reading about learners' views of matter (Driver et al., 1985; Schollum and Osborne, 1985; Andersson, 1990), particularly learners' tenacity in holding a continuous,[2] rather than particulate view of matter. As developing an understanding of atomic structure is based on a particulate view of matter, we felt a need to expose our students' views of matter.

We were also questioning the inclusion of atomic structure in the Year 10 curriculum. Why would our students want or need to know about atoms? Many of our students were not going on with chemistry, so how would the current curriculum be interesting or relevant to them? Our teaching approach was based on our belief that if students are motivated to learn, they put more thought into what they are doing, and learn in more meaningful ways. Whilst we searched for resources to help us develop a meaningful context for learning about atoms, we decided to investigate our students' views of matter.

We began with students writing and drawing about their thinking concerning air in a flask before and after some of the air had been removed (Nussbaum, 1985).

Pippa—class journal
Thank goodness we didn't start with the model of the atom! Just like states of matter it assumes a particulate picture of matter as a starting point. But, as warned in Children's Science [Gilbert and Watts, 1983; Gunstone, 1994], we *can't* assume that at all! I thought they were supposed to have covered this in Years 7 and 8, but you'd never know it.

10R *seemed* to have hardly any continuous pictures after the probe, but as soon as we started to talk about what might be between the 'dots', they were breaking out in continuous explanations all over the place!

From an examination of their responses and the following discussion, it was obvious that many of the students in our two Year 10 classes demonstrated a continuous idea of matter, despite having covered 'states of matter' at least twice in junior Science. Pippa's observations highlight an important aspect of our learning about our teaching. It would have been easy to assume that our students did have the prerequisite knowledge if we were using only one source of information—their drawings—as a guide. Encouraging the students to explain the thinking behind their drawings showed us that there were inconsistencies between what they said and what they had drawn. This experience reinforced the need for us to make a conscious, planned effort to probe their thinking in a variety of ways and to build as accurate a picture as we could of our students' thinking. It was an experience that brought home to us the (un)reality of assumed progression that much Science curriculum is based on.

We needed to rethink what to teach and how to teach it in a way that would promote meaningful learning. However, we could not assume that our teaching could bring *every* student to a particulate view of matter. Although this appears self-evident, coming to understand much more deeply the implications of gauging the progress of *individual* students and recognising the 'big comfortable lie' that much curricular progression rests on was a big shift.

Mandi—journal

The biggest shift [in thinking about student learning] for me has been in scrapping any assumptions I had about the whole group moving *en masse*. It's a big lie. It's important to 'pick on' individuals (in the nicest possible way) to understand where they're at. I understand concepts in much greater depth than before because we're going slowly and coming at them again and again. If it is so for me then surely it must be the same for my students.

We found that exposing these various assumptions—that students bring appropriate prerequisite knowledge; that the curriculum is meaningful and useful; and that teaching results in all students learning what the teacher intends—challenges the accepted way of working and carries a heavy responsibility for change.

PUT THE LID BACK ON (IT'S TOO TRICKY)

Snapshot 2: Recognising the responsibility

Mandi—journal

It's like we've opened Pandora's box. What are we supposed to do now?

Having lifted the lid on our students' learning, we were faced with a scary realisation: how should we deal with what we found? The probe and our subsequent student discussions revealed their lack of understanding of a fundamental scientific idea. It was clear that telling students the *answer* did little to change their views. We needed to find ways to help our students restructure their thinking in line with more scientifically acceptable explanations (Needham, 1987). However, we did not really understand the enormity of this task until we were immersed in and confronted by it. We had begun the unit curious to see what our students were thinking; now we suddenly realised the significance of our actions: we asked students to expose their thinking and did not know how to help them rearrange their beliefs.

Accepting responsibility meant that we needed to create a curriculum that was responsive to the particular needs of our students. This raised immediate and considerable problems for us.

DIAGNOSIS IS EASY, WHERE'S THE REST?

Snapshot 3: The research knowledge we need is missing

From the outset we were keen to draw on research to inform our teaching. Our Monash University experiences had been significant in influencing our views and we saw value in accessing the possibilities that a conceptual change approach might have on students' learning (Posner et al., 1982; Osborne and Freyburg, 1985; Driver, 1994; Gunstone, 1994). However, when we turned to the research literature to find a context for teaching about atomic structure, or practical classroom assistance for dealing with the particular conceptions we had uncovered and wanted to challenge, we found little.

Mandi—journal
This is so frustrating!! I can find probes of students' conceptions all over the place [in the research literature] but there's nothing really that says what to do next!! Bits and pieces, nothing more
. . . more than half the class has got a continuous model of matter

and we've found experiences to challenge that, but where to now? What about the kids who already have a coherent model of matter, what can they be doing? How do we get to atoms? I feel angry that the very approach that is being advocated in the literature has nothing to help implement it beyond a probe or some general description of a conceptual change classroom!

This frustration persisted throughout many of the units we taught. Probes of children's conceptions of scientific phenomena and descriptions and analyses of the shortcomings of much classroom Science teaching were abundant, but there was little to support a conceptual change approach to the teaching of whole Science units. We needed a user-friendly guide (where the users were teachers like us) for dealing with the variety of individual conceptions—how to challenge; what to do with those students who already had a coherent view of the phenomenon; what the likely response to various situations might be; good teaching procedures targeting particular concepts (e.g. POE, White and Gunstone, 1992).

Our only alternative was to invent a curriculum that was specific to our own and our students' needs. While we strongly supported the idea that teachers *should* be responsible for curriculum development and that it should be responsive to particular students' needs, our experiences led us to understand that it is a big, complex, time- and resource-demanding task. To be able to implement a conceptual change approach requires expertise in both subject matter knowledge and in the construction of learning experiences. We found it frustrating and very time consuming trying to devise a sequence of lessons to address alternative conceptions and to lead students towards a concept of the atom.

Pippa—journal

It is sort of a case of deciding what the crucial question to deal with *now* is and then finding/inventing teaching sequences that deal with clearing up that question *but* at the same time it's important to keep on referring back to, using and consolidating the concepts that have already been 'dealt with', or else they get dropped in the approach to the next bit.

Mandi—journal

I'm making a conscious, planned effort to translate theory into practice. That's draining ... We have spent so long talking about how to put theory into practice, and actually translating it is difficult. It's time consuming and frustrating. That all sounds negative. There is great stuff too. Talking at length, in depth about specific strategies and goals is fantastic; personally fulfilling.

Many of our conversations highlighted the considerable research/ practice gap. We often wondered how many other teachers like ourselves were struggling in the semi-darkness, inventing curriculum 'on the run'. A dilemma that emerged for us was that recording teaching sequences and useful conceptual conflict activities often killed them on the page—they lost the responsiveness with which they were created.

EXPOSING THEMSELVES—WHY WOULD THEY BOTHER?

Snapshot 4: Building an atmosphere of trust

Pippa—journal

We should definitely do the syringe activity from the Nussbaum (1985) chapter like we planned—hopefully one of them will come up with the same kind of idea that he suggests. It's helpful—and at least the last sub-heading says 'towards an effective teaching strategy' ... It asserts that the 'exposing event' is necessary—students must take an explicit position— i.e. make their existing conception clear—before a 'discrepant event' will lead them to sense a real conflict and hence initiate any conceptual change. So it supports getting students to publicly articulate their position ... I still think it is a big ask getting students to put their own ideas up for scrutiny. Any ideas about how to run the syringe activity sensitively?

We offered the students examples of different 'super-magnified' pictures of air and asked how they might test which was correct:

Look in a book . . .

Dye the gas . . .

Pump in water . . .

They were not short of ideas. We were able to use syringes to see if we could 'squash' air—the students felt that what they observed was closest to representation number 3 (that air is made up of small 'bits' or particles). Then . . .

Pippa—class journal
Then we had a great discussion about what's in the gaps [between particles of air] . . .

I was trying really hard to get people to put all ideas on the table—not being very kind to those who just sat there and, when pushed, said 'don't know'. Told them to try and squeeze some thoughts and ideas out.

Elena: 'This is silly I know—but something squashy? . . .' She is really searching her head for ideas, and she is so brave and self-conscious about putting them out there. I tried to use the image of foam or a sponge—why is it squashy? 'Because it's got gaps with air in them that can be squeezed out.' It feels like a bit of a circular argument though—in this case the air is analogous to nothing.

'Gases' moved toward 'space' and I left them to think about 'What is space?' tonight.

Trying to teach for conceptual change involves a cultural shift. We had reached a point in our teaching where we perceived the benefits of exploring ideas and comparing models of explanation, and we had each other to confirm the value of what we were doing in our risk-taking. But it was a difficult cultural shift for the students. The vulnerability involved in students putting ideas up for public scrutiny is real. It is a tenet of conceptual-change teaching that a learner's personal understandings must be uncovered and brought to the surface in order for a teaching event to contribute to the reconstruction of those ideas. But why would a student want to reveal their own ideas in order to have them exposed as inadequate at some later stage? Why not leave that risky stuff to others and wait for the 'right answer' to be revealed? It is a dilemma.

Acknowledging and validating the effort and difficulties associated with changes in thinking became an important part of the way that we worked with our students. This was not contained in any of the *exposing events* or *conceptual conflict* references that we read (nothing about trust, vulnerability or feelings there) and we needed to build a climate in which students were prepared to expose their *raw* thoughts and could constructively criticise the thoughts of others. We did this by encouraging students to see that the process that they were engaging in was akin to the way scientists construct science knowledge. We also provided specific opportunities for students to compare and examine how their own ideas changed during the course of instruction, and we linked assessment to this process.

Most importantly, though, we consistently and lavishly offered praise and encouragement and expressed admiration when students risked putting their ideas up for scrutiny. We tried to model risk-taking ourselves, through questioning one another in front of the students, or admitting to be confused by an idea. Thinking out loud was praised and, through the use of 'thinking pages',[3] 'thinking out loud in private' was given explicit value as an assessment goal. This was important for those students who found asking questions and revealing thoughts just too uncomfortable, even in a supportive classroom culture.

Over the course of a year, there was a marked increase in students' readiness to discuss the ideas offered and to offer reasons for their thinking, or to explain why they changed their minds about something.

'THINKING HURTS'—WHY WOULD THEY BOTHER?

Snapshot 5: Fruitfulness

Mandi—journal
We want kids to value *everything* that we do, not just identify

individual pieces that 'count'. How do we do this? We thought that by responding in writing with questions, suggestions and comments on their work, and providing opportunities for them to respond to *our* comments, that the learning would become as relevant as the marks. For some kids it has, whereas for others our comments are overlooked or neglected and their work is just a shabby mess . . .

Have just undergone a gruelling week of report writing. Idealism took a leap out of the window on Friday as Pip and I struggled with practicalities such as deadlines.

Operating a classroom in a manner that is responsive to the ideas and questions that arise is an unpredictable process and teaching sequences can easily become messy affairs. We learnt painfully that it is vital to build bridges from both ends. The students needed closure on some ideas in order to have a sense of progression. We felt reluctant to hand out 'the right answer' and did not want the class to feel that, if they did not bother, eventually we would do the thinking for them. Progress was often made in moving towards an idea but it was still frustrating for many students. We developed some thinking and assessment tasks that encouraged them to review their progress, but needed to work hard to end the lesson neatly, rather than messily interrupting a class discussion that raged on after the bell.

We needed to devise assessment tasks that clearly valued the kinds of learning that we wanted to take place in our class. It was important to assess for understanding rather than reverting to assessment for factual recall and superficial learning. We found out (through near-mutiny) that often those students who were usually successful Science learners were most resistant to this upheaval in the expectations of learning in our Science classroom. Paradoxically, these same students most often showed good conceptual understanding and became more comfortable with asking questions and examining their ideas but resented not being able to achieve 100 per cent on a test by simply swotting up the night before.

We asked the students to think hard about the concept of *nothing* between particles. One activity involved mixing liquids together with the resultant volume being less than the sum of its parts. We asked students to explain this surprising observation using the unobservable scientific model that we wanted them to accept. Again, students bravely argued against such an idea, and we continually agreed that it was very hard to imagine. Knowing what the scientific view was and being partially convinced of it rather surprisingly led to some pleasant reinforcement that they *were* learning something.

Mandi—journal
On the train to school, Gulshan asked her cousin (doing Year 12 [final year of secondary school] Chemistry) what air was made of. Her cousin said lots of different kinds of atoms. So Gulshan asked her what is in between the atoms . . . and her cousin didn't know! I'm sure Gulshan was very polite about it—but she was also pretty amazed. I got the impression that when she told her cousin that it was absolutely nothing her cousin wasn't convinced. Rather than being shaken by this, though, I think G. was feeling a bit smug!

Pippa—journal
Lots of moans today that R's class are doing lots of chemical reactions and how come we aren't, etc. I said: 'But we've been working really hard with some difficult ideas.' More whining. Anyway later in the day Karen and co. told me that they'd asked some of the kids in 10C what matter was made of and that they didn't know!

SORTING OUT WORDS AND MEANING

Snapshot 6: Learning to clearly 'speak'

Mandi—class journal
Lyn kept wanting to use the words 'absorb' and 'melt into' for the particles mixing. Lots of them say melt to describe dissolving. I think using the balls/drawing helps them to have a way of showing what they mean, but then it's sticking words on this, and helping them find appropriate words, that is hard. And it's

even harder getting them to pinpoint the meaning that we're using for words that they use in other ways.

We worked hard at encouraging students to explain their thoughts, took time to try to establish shared understanding for new language (e.g. molecule, element) and for everyday language that held assumed and different meanings (e.g. melt). It was important to us to not only know what our students were thinking but also to hear and challenge each other's thinking and to demonstrate to the students that we were all participating in the process of developing meaning. We were sensitive to the noises that sound scientific (Carr et al., 1994; Sutton, 1996) and tried not to overlay what we wanted students to say, rather taking time to really explore meaning. We had numerous experiences whereby taking time revealed language-based reasons for student confusion with Science ideas.

We felt that students needed lots of opportunities to talk about their thinking—tentative, exploratory, hypothetical talk. We encouraged them to 'tell us a bit more about what you mean', or to paraphrase what another student said. Through spending time sharing and negotiating meaning, we were able to draw links between the nature of our class discussions and the ways in which meaning is constructed and knowledge is shared in the broader scientific community. It was our intention to help students to develop a sense of the socially constructed nature of scientific knowledge and to build a picture of science as human-centred and evolving.

'LAST LESSON LAURA MADE THE POINT . . .'

Snapshot 7: Learning to really listen

Mandi—class journal
10R: Water boiling POE[4] today—discussion really interesting . . .
Kim: Maybe it [water] separates into the H and O gases then recombines again and that's why you feel the water droplets on your hand if you put your hand over it.

Laura: But when we see the pics in the book it says solids 'break up' into liquids, so then the liquid also 'breaks up' into a gas, therefore H_2O breaks up into H + O.

Beth: Yeah, and when we did the role-play about ice melting and water boiling we all had to break apart and run around the room then (she looked pretty smug). [A problem I'd never thought of before but which seems pretty obvious now it's pointed out.]

There wasn't time to work through all of this but what *I love* is that they are fighting for those models, and coming up with ideas to defend them as hard as they can. *Lots* of thinking . . .

You've got 10R next—you need to:

- acknowledge Kim's observation and deal with it (no H or O found by testing);
- introduce term 'molecule' as the smallest bit of water and link that back to the role-play (i.e. acknowledge Beth's point and help them understand that the people were molecules/smallest bits).

A prerequisite to gaining an accurate picture of what a learner is thinking involves learning to listen. If a student asks a question, and the teacher inadvertently responds to what is really a different question, it is dissatisfying and embarrassing for the student to pursue it further. Clarifying the meaning of a question or comment and moving beyond a student's initial response is important. As a teaching team, this was easier together than alone as we could ask each other (in front of the class) to clarify or explain something, or say: 'I think Sarah is actually asking . . . is that right, Sarah?' These were important instances of modelling careful listening.

In the example above, Beth was listening to Laura (with glee!) and both explained the classroom experiences they'd had that supported a model of water boiling. Kim was linking real world experiences to her alternative explanation of what was happening. Mandi needed to communicate accurately their comments to Pippa: challenging the notion that molecules break apart during boiling needed to be explicitly linked to these experiences for the challenge to be either credible or effective. Further, Bron highlighted a significant problem with a commonly used role-play that had never occurred to either of us. As well as acknowledging her point at the time, it was important to rectify the confusion in the next lesson by revisiting the role-play and explaining it in terms of the picture we moved to in the water boiling activity.[5]

TIE THEM TO A STRONG IDEA (AND COME BACK TO THE IDEA NOT THE LABEL)

Snapshot 8: Attaching labels

Pippa—journal
It seems that this idea of 'the smallest bit' is really the important idea to come to, and it would have been confusing talking about atoms to start with . . . It's amazing what the construction of water being made of two parts hydrogen to one part oxygen means to them—this is the best lesson I've ever had about the variety of interpretations that can fit one piece of information!

We used water boiling to get specific about particles. It is a fundamental idea: a molecule of water being the tiniest bit possible, but still made up of one atom of oxygen and two atoms of hydrogen. Hence the need for different labels: molecule; atom; compound; element. The activity, with its surrounding discussion, was a mini-version of everything about teaching and learning this kind of difficult idea. We had to get their mind-pictures out, compare and discuss them, and then propose and carry out some tests to see which version seemed to best represent water. Through this process, students arrived at a need to differentiate between the concepts of molecule and atom—long *before* applying labels to those concepts. We felt confident that by the time the new terms were used, they held fairly clear meanings in our students' minds.

In the past, we would have left it there, having seen that students could now use those terms in the right place. However, Snapshot 9 (below) showed us the danger of labels. Once handed out they can be slapped about with a good chance of landing in the right place and so cover up real possibilities for better understanding. We came to see then that assessment that asks for correct positioning of labels without manipulation of the ideas behind them assesses little of worth.

WHAT IS THE SMALLEST BIT?

Snapshot 9: Making the abstract concrete

Classroom set-up:
Beaker of water boiling out the front.
Instructions to student pairs:
Draw big pictures that show what happens as water boils.
Be ready to demonstrate your understanding to me using Lego.

Pippa—class journal
10R: The girls worked in pairs with felt markers on butcher's paper. They started off working on their explanations on the butcher's paper but eventually everyone had their Lego going to help them work out what the pictures actually should be. I'm sure it helps their thinking to be able to manipulate a model *while* they are trying to put snapshots of it down on paper. I'm sure that's a big problem with lots of the diagrams they get to see—it's hard to think about what's happened for one diagram to move on to the next.

The best bit was that working through the boiling water scenario with particular pairs of students (Tania and Nat were struggling) led to me asking them to use the Lego to show the smallest bit of water they could possibly get. Then asking which of the terms (atom, molecule, compound, element) we could use to describe it. It was *really powerful* for several students. 'Is this still water?' or 'What have I got now?' when I broke up the molecule. 'Show me an atom of water', '... a molecule of an element', '... an atom of a compound', '... the smallest bit of an element', etc. It was easy to see which bits particular students were having trouble with.

In our work with two different year levels, a regular theme was to explore either how Science ideas were arrived at (with supplied reasons), or how they changed over time (looking at what caused one idea to be abandoned or modified). This went hand in hand with exposing students' ideas around a particular Science concept, and then exploring those ideas and testing them in order to move towards the idea that was most scientifically acceptable. Why might people have thought that? What caused X to change their picture? Which of these pictures fits best with these results?

This problem of the unobservables (Osborne and Freyburg, 1985) permeated the whole middle school Science curriculum. Many of the ideas we were asking students to engage with were abstract (e.g. atoms, forces) or barely visible (e.g. genes, germs). We needed to find ways to help students develop sound mental representations of these ideas through somehow making them concrete. We found that asking students to express their thinking using a variety of media (e.g. 3D construction materials, drawing, writing, role-play) was helpful for this purpose.

Pippa—class journal (following year)
Affro was really struggling to get these ideas straight in her head. As I quizzed her I became aware of two things—she was obviously struggling with getting straight what happens as the water boils, and she was feeling embarrassed and uncomfortable at having this struggle witnessed by two student-teachers who were watching silently. So I said to one of them: here, you explain what happens. This girl had *great difficulty* in adequately showing what was happening [as water boils] and Affro and Claire ended up explaining to her and the chap how it worked—they got there by recognising what the university girl was doing wrong [which was of course breaking the bits apart as the water boils]! It gave me a great chance to push the 'see this is really difficult, especially as we can't actually see it' line. Ask Affro about it tomorrow.

TAKING TIME AND MAKING LINKS

Snapshot 10: Revisitation

Mandi—class journal
10G: Mixing Liquids activity brought us back to discussion of

movement of particles again. Great to see some students using their notes to try to explain their thinking. Tammie can *articulate* her difficulties now—big improvement.

For tomorrow—can you specifically set them to reflect on how their ideas have changed as a result of this activity, compared to when they did the survey?

Pippa—class journal
Hard to get them settled but eventually quiet, thoughtful writing. They are rarely asked to do this. We need to encourage them to see the value of examining their own thoughts and thinking back by themselves over previous lessons.

This was an instance where a simple task helped clarify ideas because the instructions forced students to be thoughtful. We learnt how repeatedly coming back to one idea or situation from different directions is more useful (for learning) than flitting on to a completely different example that may well cover the same ground. It is a case of limiting the variables. Either keep the situation/example/instance the same and do different things with it (e.g. water boiling: drawing; testing; explaining; etc.), or keep the representation/task the same and apply it to different instances (e.g. using lots of different-sized balls to represent particles: applying this to several different mixing activities and changes of state).

We learnt that taking plenty of time and providing continual opportunities to make links to other experiences were essential elements of classroom practice.

WRAPPING THINGS UP . . .

Changes in our practice

There are two stages necessary for teaching to take place in the ways we described and set out to achieve:

1. The teacher must believe that a constructivist or conceptual change approach is desirable.

2. The teacher must be able to develop their practice in order to teach in this way.

In this chapter we have taken the first stage as a given and have been principally concerned with exploring facets of the second stage.

We have attempted to tease out and make explicit the elements of teaching practice vital to a conceptual-change classroom. Without developing these elements and putting them consistently into practice, we believe it is not possible to explore science ideas with students in ways likely to lead to good conceptual understanding for the majority of students.

Were we successful and how do we know?

We did not set out to prove that our approach was a better way of teaching, but we do claim to have isolated and explored some of the factors that make it easier. The learning felt better—there was much discussion and writing that questioned ideas and assumptions; students generally became better at explaining the reasons underpinning their responses; we understood concepts better ourselves and our students were demonstrating that they understood them too and were prepared to give reasons to support their answers. The factors we have outlined in this chapter made this practice much smoother. When any of these factors were not practised consistently, the 'classroom culture' seemed to lose purpose; hence fruitfulness (Posner et al., 1982) can be a tenuous thing!

Pondering further—a model for this approach

Teaching involves regular reassessment of progress if it is to genuinely be responsive to the thoughts, ideas and questions of the learners. During and after lessons, teachers need to reconsider and reflect on the ways in which their learners are responding to the subject matter. The elements of classroom practice that we have described in this chapter obviously impact on what those responses will be like—and careful 'listening' is vital.

We liken this process to a cycle (see Figure 11.1) but recognise that it can be a gruelling and time-consuming process—particularly in a vacuum of suitable shared ideas and resources. Conditions that affected this approach (for us) are addressed below.

ENHANCERS

Collaboration

We would assert that our learning about our teaching was substantially enhanced by working together. It is difficult to 'see' your practice when working alone. Much has been written about the value of regularly engaging in critical reflection (Baird and Mitchell, 1986; Brookfield, 1995; Loughran, 1996) and we believe that reflection on practice is most fruitful when it is a shared process, more so when the teaching practice is also shared.

We could examine both successes and failures together; talk them through; encourage each other to persist; and affirm our purposes. This allowed negative experiences (and there were plenty) to become learning experiences, without quite as much discomfort as when borne alone. Working together forced us to think things through out loud and helped us to be more aware of, and responsive to, what was going on in our classroom.

Readiness to risk-take (and a context that allows it)

There were parallels throughout the experience between our students' learning and our own learning. We were encouraging students to task risks and we were taking risks ourselves. We tried to make explicit what we were doing and why, and we asked students to continually examine *their thinking*.

Talking things through was an essential part of our practice. If we had to explain or 'teach' something to the other, it was an explicit process and enhanced our teaching of the same idea to our students. We all learnt to listen carefully to each other.

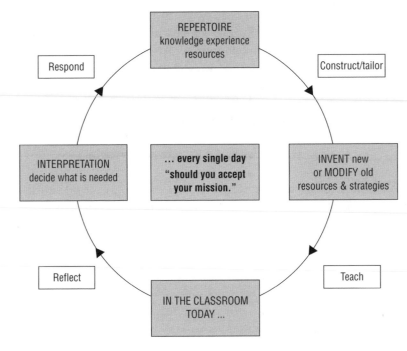

Figure 11.1: The daily cycle

A rich context

Much of our work was influenced by what we read about Children's Science and models of learning. Our connection with Monash University was the starting point for our exposure to much of this kind of information, and ready access to people and materials was invaluable. Mandi also worked part-time in teacher preparation at university, concurrent with her classroom teaching, and just as she found at university, so we found at school: that the more we experienced helping students to make better sense of their Science learning, the easier and more 'normal' this mode of practice became for us.

A supportive environment

We worked in a school situation which was relatively free from curricular constraints. The school's administration was supportive, in particular the principal (who had given us the opportunity to work together). Most importantly, the teacher in charge of the Science faculty shared our beliefs, supported our teaching practice, and continually encouraged us to record and attempt to represent for others what we were doing in the classroom.

FRUSTRATORS

Lack of appropriate support materials

We were working to a theoretical model of how we might initiate conceptual change in the classroom. This framework became as much the source of our frustration as our inspiration. We did find analyses critical of the kinds (or lack) of learning common in many Science classrooms; generalised models of constructivist teaching sequences; and some diagnostic tools to expose students' thinking. But there were no relevant classroom translations of a conceptual-change approach—resources that specifically addressed the kinds of engagement with content necessary for this kind of teaching were almost non-existent.

Difficulty in 'building the bridges'

We needed to be organised enough to 'build the bridges from both ends'. We needed to know where we were going and how we were going to assess and report students' progress. Such planning requires knowledge of the content and experience in teaching it in that way so that assessment is responsive to the students' learning experiences. The school's descriptive goal-based assessment format meant we had to find ways to bridge the gap between the classroom and the school reports.

Student attitudes to an approach that was not widespread

It was frustrating that many of the students were not ready to be more active in their learning. We failed to anticipate how difficult changing this could be (for some) and how much resentment could be incurred. Through the curriculum we devised and implemented, we intended to assist our students to become better processors of Science knowledge, to learn to identify and explain their thinking in relation to Science ideas presented and to be able to explore and express their thinking in a variety of ways. These changes were ambitious, as we wanted to change a well-established classroom culture.

> When a major classroom change is confined to just a few periods a week, students can easily dismiss this change as an idiosyncratic oddity of the teacher, and thus find a way of ignoring the change (Gunstone, 1992, p. 288).

Our expectation of the classroom as a place where students could take responsibility and were required to think hard and challenge their assumptions, at times appeared to them to be an experiment. Openly stating that we were trying something new prompted one student to comment: 'It's like we're guinea pigs for next year.' We realise now that we needed to move gradually and make much smaller changes.

WHERE TO FROM HERE?

Conditions that enhance rather than frustrate the process make an enormous difference. Neither of us could now contemplate teaching otherwise as, through the unusually supportive nature of our collaboration, we have had time to find ways of doing and to normalise these elements of our practice. This is not to say that teaching in this way has become easy. Our experiences should be of interest to teacher educators who propose a constructivist approach to their student teachers, as the conditions to support such an approach, generally do not get as much attention as the constructivist model itself.

Representing teaching strategies and approaches so that the reasons for using them are explicit to others matters, yet a chapter such as this does not help in the ways we initially anticipated—to share this knowledge so that it is a less gruelling task for others. The responsive, and therefore highly personalised, nature of this approach to teaching makes the production and sharing of such resources a difficult task.

In some ways, we feel uncomfortable that this chapter may not specifically help other teachers who are working at developing teaching for conceptual change. In our attempt to frame our practice, this account might ring true with others as the practice of teaching Science in a constructivist manner, focusing on developing conceptual understanding in students, is a messy and muddy business, but one that feels exciting and worthwhile. It is truly the *swamp of real practice* (Flack et al., 1999).

The exchanges we have enjoyed have been a vital ingredient in developing our teaching.

Pippa—journal

I keep thinking about what you said about making the abstract concrete. You're right—genes, forces, germs, atoms—they're all invisible. And the Year 10s have had the lot this year. I have to remember to keep explicitly referring to how hard this is. When you were talking them through the mixing activities you kept doing this—sort of giving them permission to find things difficult; letting Elena know that you expect her to find this difficult, that *you* find it difficult. I realise now how important that is—not only does it lessen the 'dumb' feeling when you can't 'get it', but it encourages the students to share their thinking and take bigger risks in thinking out loud. I'm sure that this means a more honest classroom—I certainly feel as though I have a better handle on where people are in their thinking. And the other thing that occurred to me about it is that when they do 'get' something publicly recognised as being difficult, surely they will value that learning more? . . . Life would certainly be much simpler if we could pretend that everybody understood what we told them . . .

NOTES

1. We maintained a communication book (referred to in this chapter as *class journal*) for each class about the daily 'goings on'. In addition we found it necessary to start a *journal* for more wide-ranging written conversations.

2. The notion that all matter is made of particles is fundamental to modern science. In a continuous model of matter, there are no separate particles.

3. We continually encouraged students to express ideas, thoughts, puzzlement and questions on the left-hand page of their exercise books. The body of their work continued on the right-hand side. This also allowed us to comment and ask for clarification and reasons next to their answers, with plenty of space for the required responses from them. For some students, the 'thinking page' became an ongoing dialogue where they pursued ideas and pondered 'what-ifs' in great depth. Others did not warm to this more informal work at all, and only wrote the bare minimum in response to occasional 'left-hand page tasks'.

4. At the start of this Predict Observe Explain activity, students are asked to look at a beaker of water and draw a picture of what the water would look like if they had their super-magnifying glasses on and could see how the hydrogen and oxygen were arranged to make up water. The water is then heated until boiling and students are then asked to look at steam coming from the top of the beaker and draw a picture of the water boiling—what do students think happens as the water boils and turns into a gas?

   Using student models, the class predicts whether a test will indicate the presence of hydrogen gas or not (and similarly for oxygen). The results are used to decide which student drawings are most appropriate for boiling water.

5. In the role-play, students are asked to take the role of the particles of a solid as it is heated. The particles separating as the role-play shifts from solid to liquid to gas are in fact the smallest bits of water—i.e. the molecules, not the atoms. This incident with Bron helped confirm our belief that it is problematic to begin this

topic by introducing atoms, as they are not generally the smallest naturally occurring bits of anything.

REFERENCES

Andersson, B. (1990). Pupils' Conceptions of Matter and Its Transformations (Age 12–16). *Studies in Science Education*, 18, 53–85.

Baird, J.R. and Mitchell, I.J. (1986). *Improving the Quality of Teaching and Learning: An Australian Case Study—the PEEL Project.* Melbourne: PEEL Publishing.

Brookfield, S.D. (1995). *Becoming a Critically Reflective Teacher.* San Francisco: Jossey-Bass.

Carr M., Barker, M., Bell, B., Biddulph, F., Jones, A., Kirkwood, V., Pearson, J. and Symington, D. (1994). The Constructivist Paradigm and Some Implications for Science Content and Pedagogy. In P. Fensham, R. Gunstone and R. White (eds), *The Content of Science: A Constructivist Approach to its Teaching and Learning.* London: Falmer Press, 147–60.

Driver, R. (1994). Theory into Practice II: A Constructivist Approach to Curriculum Development. In P. Fensham (ed.), *Developments and Dilemmas in Science Education.* London: Falmer Press, 133–49.

Driver, R., Guesne, E. and Tiberghien, A. (eds) (1985). *Children's Ideas in Science.* Buckingham: Open University Press.

Flack, J., Osler, J. and Mitchell, I. (1999). Mapping the Swamp: A Case Study of Reflective Practice. In J.R. Baird (ed.), *Reflecting, Teaching, Learning: Perspectives on Educational Improvement.* Melbourne: Hawker Brownlow, 35–56.

Gilbert, J. and Watts, M. (1983). Conceptions, Misconceptions and Alternative Conceptions: Changing Perspectives in Science Education. *Studies in Science Education*, 10, 61–98.

Gunstone, R. (1992). A Tertiary Educator's View. In J.R. Baird and J.R. Northfield (eds) (1992). *Learning from the PEEL Experience.* Melbourne: PEEL Publishing.

—— (1994). Learners in Science Education. In P. Fensham (ed.), *Developments and Dilemmas in Science Education.* London: Falmer Press, 73–95.

Loughran, J.J. (1996). *Developing Reflective Practice: Learning About Teaching and Learning Through Modelling.* London: Falmer Press.

Needham, R. (1987). *Teaching Strategies for Developing Understanding in Science.* Leeds: Children's Learning in Science Project, University of Leeds.

Nussbaum, J. (1985). The Particulate Nature of Matter in the Gaseous Phase. In R. Driver, E. Guesne and A. Tiberghien (eds) (1985). *Children's Ideas in Science.* Buckingham: Open University Press.

Posner, G., Strike, K., Hewson, P. and Gertzog, W. (1982). Accommodation of a Scientific Conception: Towards a Theory of Conceptual Change. *Science Education.* 66 (2), 243–60.

Schollum, B. and Osborne, R. (1985). Relating the New to the Familiar. In R. Osborne and P. Freyburg, *Learning in Science. The Implications of Children's Science.* Auckland: Heinemann.

Sutton, C. (1996). Beliefs About Science and Beliefs About Language. *International Journal of Science Education,* 18 (1), 1–18.

White, R.T. and Gunstone R.F. (1992). *Probing Understanding.* London: Falmer Press.

Tales from the poppy patch

Jo Osler and Jill Flack

INTRODUCTION

We are two elementary school teachers who embarked on a teacher-research journey over six years ago. We began because we wanted to make changes in how we taught and how our students learnt. Our students appeared to see school as a series of unrelated episodes in which they had little power in the learning process. Our students were passive learners, happy for us to control and direct their learning.

We started tentatively as teacher-researchers hoping that we could formally identify, and strategically work towards, solving our teaching and learning problems. We wanted our students to be more meta-cognitive—to be active learners.

In this chapter, we highlight one aspect of our journey as we tell the story that we have lived as teachers researching our practice. The story focuses on the process of gaining more confidence as researchers and the subsequent changes that occurred within our classrooms.

Our journey as teacher-researchers illustrates that we cannot separate the process from the product if we truly want to understand the changes that have taken place, learn from our findings and share the wisdom we have gained. We therefore reflect on the following in this chapter:

- the factors that led us to seek change in the way we taught and the way our students approached their learning;
- the impact on our colleagues and ourselves as we became keen observers of our own practice and more informed and strategic in the way we addressed issues of teaching and learning; and,
- the realisation that our journey needs to be told to help teachers and academics understand some of the complexities of being teacher-researchers.

TEACHERS . . . STORYTELLERS EXTRAORDINAIRE

We have chosen to portray our journey in the form of a story, a story that reflects both highs and lows. We hope this story goes some way towards effectively sharing our experiences. The story itself is a fable; it has a message—or in this case, lots of messages—that we encourage the reader to explore.

Our story: Tales from the poppy patch

In a small patch amongst many others grew a poppy. She had always been a happy poppy. Happy with her friends and enjoying what she did. Just the same, she was inquisitive about the way things worked in other places for other poppies. So it gave her great pleasure when another poppy who shared her curiosity began to grow right beside her. Together these two friends looked upwards and outwards from their part of the world.

It had been a great time for growing. The two poppies were thriving. They had learned to organise and manage the nutrients from the familiar, comfortable earth around them, and lately they had discovered how to get more energy and nourishment from the sun way beyond their own small patch.

The sun was available for all the poppies but sometimes the two friends needed to actively seek the best position to get the most from its rays. It surprised them a little to find that they had grown tall and that they now had a different view of things. At the same time, though, it was exciting because they could see from their poppy patch clear across to the other poppy patches that were nearby. The poppies over there looked much the same but different enough for them to wonder about what they did and how they got to be that way. The two poppies discovered that they could be seen by the poppies from the other patch and that they could call out and ask them questions. The distant poppies were generous about sharing their different knowledge and they would respond and give them great insights about their world. It was interesting and stimulating and gave the two friends plenty to talk about and reflect on. Life in their own patch now became more interesting because they could see it through different eyes.

On the other hand, their old friends in their poppy patch looked just as they always had and sometimes the two poppies forgot that others didn't know what they knew and couldn't see what they saw, and that was why they couldn't be any different.

Now unfortunately, because the poppies were tall, they didn't have the support of the bunch around them; they felt fragile and very vulnerable to the elements. The whispering breezes from all directions seemed extra strong as they blew across the poppy patch where they stood so tall. At times they even feared that the pressure of the winds would cause them to snap and break. They called for help but their old friends couldn't hear them because they were used to them being so far away and they didn't expect them to need their help anyway! Their new friends were not able to help them much from where they were; though they did offer encouragement. The two poppies began to envy the safety and security that staying with the bunch would have given them, but of course they couldn't go back.

Despite the frustration and sadness they felt when they thought of their friends and what they were missing out on, the tall poppies celebrated the many joys that their growth was giving them. They were determined to remain patient, knowing that one day they would share their new insights with their old friends. They believed that eventually many would seek the light and view from where they were, especially when they realised that growing tall was not undesirable.

Time passed and their earlier fragility lessened as they gained strength and became tougher. They noticed that some other poppies in other parts of the patch were taller and because of where those poppies grew and what their views were, it made the patch far more interesting.

The winds no longer frightened them as they had. One day in a particularly strong wind, the two poppies commented on how strong they felt and wondered why that was. They looked around and to their delight, right next to them, were some other poppies. Some of them they knew, some of they didn't, but they all could share the vision of what was beyond their poppy patch. They too were thriving.

The two poppies were excited at their excitement and at last they could talk and share and support more of their kind. Best of all, they could see more together. Perhaps their message had not fallen on deaf ears after all. Surely the winds could not knock down a whole bunch of poppies!

REVEALING THE POPPY SECRETS!

Our intention, then, is to draw from the poppy patch fable the important aspects of our journey.

Fertile ground

We did not realise that we had embarked on a journey until we were well past the point of no return. We found ourselves changing quickly, but the events which marked the many stages of our journey are clear.

It was not all smooth sailing, but the knowledge and skills we have gained have made it well worth the effort and stress.

Our journey is about two teachers who grew to be teacher-researchers—two teachers who learnt to describe what affected them in their time of growing. The conditions were right, the ground was fertile and ' . . . *together these friends looked upwards and outward from their part of the world*'.

Working together was a most significant event in our professional careers. We established a working relationship built on trust, respect, common beliefs about teaching and learning, and a shared desire to become more effective classroom teachers. We also shared concerns about our students and the way they approached their learning in our classrooms. An early defining moment was a simple conversation we had with our students. It turned out to be an eye-opening experience that provided us with insights into how our students viewed school.

A *defining moment*

'What is the curriculum?' I asked the two Grade 5 classes. 'A day off!' chorused several students. 'When we stay home, but the teachers have to come!' added someone else, while many other students nodded in agreement.

'OK then.' I pressed on, 'Why do you think students come to school?' Again our students were quick to answer. They were confident they knew the answers to these very straightforward questions.

'To get a good job!'

'To see your friends.'

'To learn things.'

Some of the students came to school because no one was home.

'I can't stay home, my parents work.'

A couple of students thought they had no alternative.

'It's the law!'

Really, no arguing with that!

'OK then, what is the teacher's role?' Silence—this one

stumped them. Students had a great deal of trouble explaining their thoughts, until one piped up with: 'Kids come to school, so teachers can get paid, that's their job!'

Jo and I looked at each other; this incredible interaction had confirmed our suspicions that some of the critical components of school were a complete mystery to the students (Osler and Flack, 2000).

From our discussion, we were able to draw a number of conclusions (Flack and Osler, 2000) about how we believed our students viewed school:

- Students are often unclear about what school can offer them. They feel as though they are expected to attend so they can get a job and because it is the law.
- School is a series of unrelated episodes.
- Students have little or no power in the learning process—school is done *to* them, *by* teachers, for their own good.
- The curriculum is a collection of subject areas and facts.
- Daily lessons just happen with little or no thought or preparation from teachers.
- School is independent of the 'real' world.
- If students did not attend school, teachers would not get paid.

As a result of this rich student–teacher exchange, we became determined to demystify school and the learning process.

Our working relationship became a partnership. We had redefined our beliefs and were becoming more strategic in the way we approached our classroom practice: '... *It had been a great time for growing. The two poppies were thriving.*' It certainly was an exciting time and we were making important discoveries: '... *they had learned to organise and manage the nutrients from the familiar comfortable earth around them.*' But we wanted more. We needed answers and direction but we still did not really understand exactly what we were doing that was different, or why it was working so well.

Injection of fertiliser

Unfortunately, the normal 'grab-bag' type of professional development so commonly offered ceased to be of value to us. Such professional development simply became an array of classroom activities supplemented by instructions. Simply 'doing' was no longer sufficient. We needed to know why students behaved in particular ways and how outcomes might change through doing things differently.

We were lucky: '. . . *they had discovered how to get more energy and nourishment from the sun, way beyond their own small patch.*' We began to look beyond the confines of the school to find the answers we now so desperately needed. We discovered PEEL (Project for the Enhancement of Effective Learning, see Baird and Mitchell, 1986; Baird and Northfield, 1992). PEEL was based on teachers' concerns about passive learning and the subsequent promotion of more purposeful, active learning. It provided us with answers to some of our questions and when we had the opportunity to join PAVOT (the Perspectives and Voice of the Teacher, see Loughran, 1999), we grabbed the chance. PAVOT aimed to assist teachers to research aspects of their practice and to get their voice into the research literature. We never realised then how important and rewarding joining the project was going to be.

We thought we knew a lot about academics, the ones who 'own the theory', who research using 'numbers and statistics'. We questioned how much they knew about the pressures of classroom teaching—harsh, but true. Our views certainly changed when we met the academics involved in PAVOT: '*We could be seen by the poppies from the other patch and could call out and ask them questions.*' Better still, they answered: '*The distant poppies were generous about sharing their different knowledge and they respond[ed] and gave insights about their world.*' They had the theory that, at this point, was beyond our reach.

Although we were many months into our research, and it was evident to us that change was taking place, the academics were able to help us understand that what we were doing was not only worthwhile, but exciting and new. Some of the insights we gained included a realisation that we were:

- encouraging students to develop strategies to remain 'on task' for extended periods of time;
- developing and using teaching strategies and procedures that encouraged students to make links in their learning;
- valuing what students brought to class and provided opportunities for them to access and use their prior knowledge; and
- doing research related to that of others who were exploring their theories of teaching and learning.

The academics not only helped us to understand the changes we had made to our teaching practice and the impact that was having on our students' learning, but offered us new ideas, explained current theories and helped us to 'frame' our practice.

Through this early period, it took a number of meetings and many hours of reflection and discussion for us to finally realise what the 'it' was that we were doing. We called our research 'it' for quite a while until we knew what we were really trying to do. In fact, we were much further along in our journey before the word 'research' comfortably rolled off our tongues.

'It' eventually got a name: 'Creating Independent Learners'. We always knew we wanted to improve student learning, but it was through the knowledge and support of our academic colleagues that we were able to be more specific about what we were trying to achieve—even ambitious to answer our questions and share our experience with others.

The semantic map (see Figure 12.1) was our first attempt at framing our classroom research and was included in our first paper published in an educational journal (Flack, Osler and Mitchell, 1995): '*It was interesting and stimulating and gave the two friends plenty to talk about and reflect on.*'

It was a time of rapid growth and at this early stage in our journey, although it was extremely satisfying, it was also professionally very demanding. We were continually being pushed out of our 'comfort zone'. Some things that we thought we had right would, upon reflection, be a catalyst for further research, reflection and change. The amount of knowledge we were accumulating and generating ourselves was, to use a word from our students, awesome. Although we never

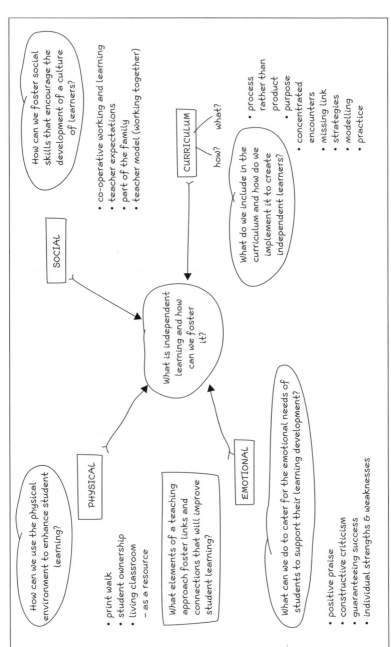

Figure 12.1: Semantic map: 'What is independent learning and how can we foster it?'

realised at the time how important that knowledge would become to us, we needed to learn how to communicate this knowledge to others.

Sharing our findings with academics was, in the beginning, mentally demanding. We quickly realised that academics and teachers have different languages. The academic language seemed to centre on theory and, although we reluctantly admit it now, it was also full of 'big', unfamiliar words. We often came away stimulated but mentally exhausted. We found ourselves trying to keep up with discussions, whilst at the same time translating academic jargon into a practical language of teaching. Now we share a language with our academic mentors that makes communication much more effective.

Thus far, our journey had certainly been more positive than negative. The negatives we now refer to as hurdles, but they did not stop us, just slowed us down. In terms of success, our teaching practice had changed and our students had become more purposeful and effective learners and our journey continued: '*Life in their own patch now became more interesting because they could see it through different eyes.*'

Unrest in the patch

Our first extended high was soon to become our first low. We knew we were developing professionally but never realised our growth was having a negative impact on '*our old friends in the poppy patch, who looked as they always had*'. They were not excited about what we were finding out. How could they be? They had not had our experiences. Sadly, this was the beginning of a professional distancing which still plagues us today. We have learnt to cope with it, but it was not always that way.

We tried to come to grips with the change and to understand it— why was it that colleagues we had worked so effectively with in the past now often appeared disinterested? '*Now because the poppies were tall, they didn't have the support of the bunch around them, they felt fragile and very vulnerable to the elements.*'

We were receiving a lot of attention and support from our academic colleagues as well as from teachers from other schools; we had introduced Open Days to our classes in order to better manage the requests from teachers and academics who wanted to see our 'independent learners' in action. We soon discovered that being different can be challenging for others and we now see that the attention we were attracting could have created instances whereby our colleagues experienced a form of professional jealousy—what made us worthy of such attention?

Within our school, our colleagues remained distant throughout this exciting yet demanding time. At the time, we could only guess at why they reacted this way. They probably felt uncomfortable about our changes. We were receiving opportunities and attention for doing what could well have been perceived as the same job as our colleagues—being classroom teachers. One result of all of this was that we were out of the school a lot more than is normal for teachers and this did not go over well with the rest of the staff.

We really felt caught in a nowhere land between school and university. We certainly had not become academics and did not wish to be, yet we felt very comfortable visiting that side of the educational world. However, we certainly felt different now and we were being treated differently. The academics, although very supportive, could not fully understand the professional distancing we were experiencing and our old teacher friends did not appreciate that we still needed their support. Perhaps to them we appeared confident. We had reached a point where we needed to decide whether to continue or stop. We held a crisis meeting to try to work through the strain we were experiencing: '*The two poppies began to envy the safety and security that staying with the bunch would have given them, but of course they couldn't go back.*'

We had learnt too much. We wanted the changes that were taking place in ourselves and in our classrooms to continue. Due to the support from our academic colleagues and the success we were experiencing in our classrooms, we continued our journey. The episodes we briefly summarise below, through vignettes, highlight the changes that were taking place in our classrooms and are indicative of the reasons why we did decide to continue our research.

Critical incidents

Each vignette carries understandings and insights into the value of what was happening to us and our students as we worked to help them become more independent and responsible learners. We had been teaching our students how to use a range of procedures that encouraged their thinking about their learning (metacognition). Our students learnt how to make choices and be in more control of their own learning. We documented 'breakthroughs'—evidence of student change that reflected the changes in our teaching.

The creative learner

Broddy, an enthusiastic six-year-old, was asked to use a procedure to show the new understandings he had developed during a unit of work on weather. Broddy, who had been busy for days working with his wind gauge (designed and built entirely by himself) had no trouble in choosing to use a labelled diagram. However, he quickly realised the limitations of the labelled diagram—it was not going to show everything he had learned, only what his wind gauge looked like. After some contemplation, Broddy approached me with his new idea. He announced to me: 'I've made up a new procedure; a labelled diagram–fact file. It has a picture and then facts around it to explain it!'

Whose learning is it? Our personal initiatives board

Once students became familiar with using the procedures, they began to use them at home. We were so pleased with their efforts that we introduced a large, gold noticeboard to display their efforts. Within days it was absolutely covered with work. Our students had not only learnt to use these procedures themselves, but they had also taught their parents, friends, brothers and sisters to use the procedures as well.

School on Saturday—who's coming?

We felt as though we had so much work to get through that we did not have enough time to do it all, so during a class meeting we jokingly asked our students to come to school on Saturday to try and catch up. The next day nearly half of our students had asked their parents about coming in on Saturday; better still, they were happy to do it.

You can't be sick in Mrs Osler's or Mrs Flack's class

On different occasions we had parents arrive at our classrooms to collect work for their students who were sick and therefore away for the day. This was certainly unusual for an absence of only one day. A few weeks later, a parent came to school with her sick child in tow and asked us to explain to Jackson that it was OK to have a day at home. Jackson would not have it. He said: 'If you miss a day you miss too many links and you won't have prior knowledge!'

Taking a break

During the year, our students had learnt to determine for themselves whether or not their learning was effective. 'Taking a break' became a common occurrence for students who felt tired whilst doing their work. In the beginning, when this was a novelty, we often had many students on a break. We had a few teething problems. However, luckily for us and our students, we moved on. Tom, a six-year-old who had up until that point been an extremely dependent learner, was seriously involved in a learning sequence. After completing a lot of writing, he told me that his hand was sore and that he had decided because he was tired that he needed to take a break.

He spent the next ten minutes enjoying a book as he perched himself in one of the beanbags. This was not so unusual, as it was something that all of our students could do. But the best part was that his effective decision-making skills did not end there. He returned to his work of his own accord, worked out where he was up to and continued to write some more and to complete his learning task.

Poppies go OS

We had entered the next phase of our journey, 'The new dawning', and never looked back. We came to see the research as just one important component of our lives, not the only one. We became more relaxed about what we were doing and for the first time we called ourselves 'teacher-researchers'. We were involved in classroom research. *We* had finally accepted where we were and what we were doing and were enjoying the intellectual challenges associated with this new era.

It was here, within the 'new dawning', that we finally understood the nature of change. To grow and change, one needs to choose to be a learner. Our early attempts at sharing our new understandings with other teachers were probably fairly threatening for them. We were so excited about our work that we could not believe that others would not want to follow in our footsteps. We thought: 'If we could do it, why couldn't they?' We now mockingly refer to these early attempts at communicating difference as 'The Jill and Jo Show'.

It was Singapore, our first overseas conference (Joint Conference of AARE [Australian Association for Research in Education] and ERA [Educational Research Association, Singapore], 1996), that made us realise that we had another story to tell. It was our first attempt at writing an academic paper on our own. It was confusing: 'What do people want to know about our work? Do they want to know about our classroom changes and successes? Or do they want to know about our journey as "teacher-researchers"?'

Professionally, the conference was very successful and reaffirmed that we did have things to say. We also learnt more about the world of academia, the need for researchers to 'get their work out there' and to be aware of the research of others. Presenting at this international conference was another valuable experience that only added to the pool of knowledge we had gained from our journey together.

Unfortunately, the experience was not all positive. To attend the conference, we needed to be away from school (again). Nobody seemed to know how this was going to be possible. The school passed it off as an Education Department concern while the Education Department did not have a budget line for such ventures. There was no precedent, so the Education Department was keen for the responsibility to remain with the school. (Yet the Education Department applauded our efforts and thought it was a great idea for us to go.) The school was not quite so positive. It was a new and different situation, one that a school would not normally face, but we really felt the lack of support. It literally took months to sort through the red tape. In the end, how we were able to go was not as important as the struggle we faced. It became clear that our education system was not well equipped to support teacher-research. Teacher-researchers are different and have different needs that will only be met if the teacher-research 'barrow' continues to be pushed.

'Breaking new ground' and 'pushing existing boundaries' have become familiar sayings for us as at times we have had to really struggle to take the next step in our journey. Singapore was definitely one of those defining experiences; unfortunately, however, at the school level it only added to the tensions we were experiencing with our colleagues.

Life back in the patch

After three more international conferences and a couple of academic papers, we now feel better able to share our stories. We have come to see the need to communicate the knowledge we have gained through writing—was that a sigh of relief from our academic colleagues?

Now we want to write. We want to share both aspects of our story. Our journey is 'two-pronged'. There is the classroom story that we are so used to telling and there is the story about us becoming teacher-researchers. We have now become more interested in sharing both stories, instead of just one: '*They believed that eventually many would seek the light and the view from where they were, especially when they realised that growing tall was not undesirable.*'

While we continued to develop and grow, we spent the next period of time consolidating what we had learnt. Consolidating meant framing our practice in ways that made it easier to communicate and share, and our research project became 'Building metacognition in young learners'. It was at this time that we also began to identify signs of growth in our colleagues. They were growing with their own ideas in their own ways, yet they were openly experimenting with some of ours. They even started to ask us questions and show interest in what we were doing—maybe even acceptance: '*They looked around and to their delight, right next to them were some poppies. Some of them they knew* . . .' For these teachers, the conditions were right, the soil was fertile and they had begun to grow: '*Perhaps our message hadn't fallen on deaf ears after all.*'

Future poppy adventures

For us, writing this chapter has been the latest, challenging step in our journey. This is a story about our professional lives and includes personal accounts of events, some of which we have previously only shared with each other. Our intention was not to point the finger and blame anyone for the negative aspects we have had to endure, only to finally share our story and encourage others to begin their own teacher-researcher journeys. Our journey does not end here, for there is still so much we have not told and more for us to discover. Our journey will go on and '. . . *together these friends*' will continue to '. . . *look upwards and outwards from their part of the world*'.

IMPORTANT ASPECTS OF THE POPPY JOURNEY

There is so much more we could unpack to further understand what has happened to us. It has certainly been an enjoyable and educational experience pulling apart the journey in order to understand these significant events. Our dilemma now is deciding which aspects are the most relevant to teachers and academics, in order to paint a clearer picture of what happens to teachers as they become teacher-researchers. We find ourselves needing to answer the questions, 'What kept us going?', 'How did we know our research was successful?', and 'How do we measure professional growth?'

None of these questions can be answered simply. Our answers, though, lie in the evidence within our 'poppy story' and in the section where we reveal our 'poppy secrets'. This evidence we like to call our 'points of consolidation'. We learnt that our greatest periods of productivity were when we were under pressure, when significant occasions effectively 'drove' us forward in our development. They represent periods of rapid growth, generally accompanied by feelings of stress and panic as we struggled to manage our new understandings, our time and our data, so that we could effectively communicate our research findings—these were 'poppies under pressure'.

It is through fully understanding these 'points of consolidation' that we can address the points raised at the beginning of this chapter. Therefore, we offer the following three major themes from our work and use examples of our points of consolidation in order to focus on the advantages of such episodes and to represent the challenges they offer to teacher-researchers.

Factors that led us to seek changes in the way we taught and the way our students approached their learning

- *1994 (February)*—Academics came to visit our classrooms to see our 'work in action'. We had never done so much preparation and reading to be 'ready for them'. In fact, many of the things we covered that day were relatively new—for them and for us. It was a huge step in our understanding of effective teaching and learning.

- *1994 (March)*—One month into our research, our first 'show and tell' session with the academics—'panic'! What will we take? What will we talk about? What will they think of us?

- *1994 (May)*—Four months into our research and the change in our classroom was rapid. The Dean of Education at Monash University invited us to take his Masters class and talk about our classrooms as examples of innovative practice. At that point we were just doing it! We had no explicit organisation or language for it. We needed to make our research manageable enough to share. We developed our first frame, categorising our practice into social-emotional, intellectual and the physical environment (refer to Figure 12.1: The semantic map).

Initial concerns we had about the way our students approached school learning led us to seek changes in the way our students learned and the way we taught. Even now, six years later, events that occur in our classrooms still drive us to seek further change—as has been the case throughout our research journey.

When the academics actually visited our classroom, it placed us under extreme pressure and triggered a period of rapid professional growth. We needed to frame our practice in order to make more sense of our research so it would be manageable and easier to share. At this stage, we were concentrating more on framing the changes in our teaching and were struggling to understand the changes in our students' approaches to learning. Here the academics helped us to better understand our practice by explaining known theory and connecting it with what we were attempting to do. Further, they shared their insights into the changes students were making in their approaches to learning: '*The distant poppies were generous about sharing their different knowledge.*'

By framing and 'making sense' of our practice, we came to understand the changes and recognise how our classrooms were different. We also came to see the impact our changes in teaching practice had on our students' learning, which provided us with a clearer direction for further research: '*Life in their own patch now became more interesting because they could see it through different eyes.*'

Impact on our colleagues and ourselves as we became observers of practice and more informed and strategic about addressing issues of teaching and learning

- *1994*—Professional writing on a small scale: our first published journal article required us to write for other educators and to make links with the literature—'a daunting task'! A new genre, an entirely new challenge.
- *1996*—Our first international conference presentation: Singapore. We had to write a paper and present our work to a different educational audience.

- Reviewing the purpose and direction of our involvement in teacher-research specifically in terms of out-of-hours work—our families met and we all discussed what we were doing and whether or not we wanted to continue.

The more we came to understand our practice, the more we wanted to communicate our practice to others. We were so excited by what we were achieving in the classroom that we thought everyone would want to know about it. Many genuinely did, but some did not. When teachers responded enthusiastically to our attempts to communicate our research, our self-esteem was boosted, and it validated for us the value of teacher wisdom: '. . . *the tall poppies celebrated the many joys that their growth was giving them and they were determined to remain patient and share their new insights.*'

It became evident that communication through writing was something we would probably have to get used to, even though we found it daunting, even threatening. This second point of consolidation made us aware of the effect our teacher-research had on others, especially our colleagues. They reacted negatively to our first opportunity to go overseas or chose to ignore what was happening to us. Few displayed interest in and support for what we were trying to do: '. . . *they didn't have the support of the bunch around them.*'

Both the positives and negatives of these first two points of consolidation were catalysts for the third. Was the price we were paying for our success too high? '*Time passed and their earlier fragility lessened as they gained strength and became tougher.*'

Although there had been major changes in terms of our immediate professional environment, peers, colleagues and students, we realised the necessity of our strong collaborative professional relationship as the cornerstone of our work. It was at this point that we entered the next phase of our journey, the 'new dawning'. This era represented a benchmark for reflection, measurement and development. We learnt to make our research more manageable and enjoyable.

Our journey needs to be told to help others understand the complexities of being teacher-researchers

• *1999*—The need to write another paper for an overseas conference—this time, the AERA (American Educational Research Association) conference held in Montreal, Canada. We realised the need to write about the teacher-research journey, not the classroom story that we had become so used to telling.

For us, this was our first real attempt at framing and understanding the journey in order to share it with others. It was not until we had attended the conference that we realised how important that task had been. It was evident that, in many ways, academics and teachers exist in very different worlds: '. . . *they could see from their poppy patch clear across to the other poppy patches.*'

It was because of this realisation that we believed our role as teacher-researchers was important in bridging the two worlds. We had established working relationships with academics and were able to share with them insights into classroom practice. However, we were still a part of the teaching world and felt we could help other teachers understand what academics had to offer. As teacher-researchers, we can access the 'knowledge and theory' academics have for other teachers and we can also help academics realise that teachers can generate their own theories and knowledge about classroom practice.

We returned from that conference wiser, as we realised that in order to share our wisdom, we had to write for a wide range of audiences—thus the poppy fable was born.

Realising the importance of identifying points of consolidation throughout our journey made the process of reflection much more effective. We have come to realise that there are other significant elements to our journey that, like our points of consolidation, have made it successful.

Poppy collaboration, within the patch and beyond

'So it gave her great pleasure when another poppy who shared her curiosity began to grow right beside her . . . The two poppies discovered that they could be seen by the poppies from the other patch and that they could call out and ask them questions.'

We learnt that collaborating with others in research is valuable and essential for growth and development. Two-way collaboration is the ideal: teacher–teacher; and teacher–academic. This type of collaboration has worked for us because both aspects of collaboration allowed daily interaction and problem-solving discussions (colleague) and ongoing 'external' mentoring and support (Table 12.1 summarises these).

Table 12.1: Benefits of collaboration

Teacher–teacher	Teacher–academic mentor
• Easier to sustain the necessary energy levels	• Validation of teachers' work beyond the classroom
• Makes taking a risk less 'risky'	• Bridges the gap between theory and practice
• Develops trusts that create a supportive environment for work	• Encourages the development of different skills—e.g. professional writing
• Shared highs and lows	• Combines the intellectual wisdom
• A 'sounding board' for ideas	• of two areas of the educational
• Different perspectives offer	world
• alternate insights	• Builds understandings and respect between the two professions

Developing the poppy environment

'They had learned to organise and manage the nutrients from the familiar, comfortable earth around them and lately they had discovered how to get more energy and nourishment from the sun, way beyond their own small patch.'

We also learnt that teacher-researchers need to create their own research environment where they can develop the knowledge and skills they need to move forward with their work (summarised in Table 12.2).

Table 12.2: Skills and research conditions for teacher-researchers

Research conditions	Skills to be developed
• *Time*: teacher-researchers need to create time to reflect on their work and to talk with colleagues	• *Reflection:* developing and valuing reflective practice
• *Links*: develop links with academics	• *Articulation*: ability to name and 'frame practice'
• *Forums*: access to various forums to share research findings	• *Familiarity with research literature*: to seek and undertake more professional reading
• *Support*: from the immediate school community	• *Linking*: learn how to link their own work to the work and theories of others
• *Systematic support*: beyond the school for sharing findings more widely—e.g. financing teacher replacement days	• *Writing*: skills of professional writing
	• *Presentations*: skills of 'presenting' to others

Our students and their parents certainly supported us, but our colleagues were not so ready, or able, to lend their support. Importantly, many people were supportive in that they believed in what we were doing, but they did not know how they could support us.

THE POPPY LEGEND: IMPLICATIONS FOR OTHER EDUCATORS

We have undertaken an intensive professional development experience. Becoming teacher-researchers has offered us hitherto hidden insights. It is no surprise that we would like to see many more teachers documenting and sharing their classroom research as the benefits are many. However, teachers need to 'own' the research if they are to commit themselves to pursuing answers to 'their' questions and 'sustain' the research over time. They need to be sure there is something in it for them.

From our experience, the critical factors that we believe need to be in place to ensure a productive period of research include teacher-researchers:

- being part of a convened group—teachers new to research need to be invited to explore the possibilities of undertaking classroom research;
- beginning with concerns or questions about their classroom practice that they wish to explore;
- working collaboratively—their projects may be different, but they need to have a close working relationship with a colleague to encourage progress; ideally, they would be friends, but essentially they need to share some common ground or educational philosophy;
- ideally being geographically located near to each other so that frequent and easy access is possible;
- being supported by academics who can mentor and enhance their progress;
- having a minimum level of support within their school from their principal and colleagues, though they also need support from outside their school—but within the system in which they work; and,
- working towards an event that requires them to share their work—for example, writing, presenting, etc. A little bit of pressure seems to bring out the best.

THE POPPIES' LAST WORD

The process of researching became as enriching to our practice as the knowledge we were generating from our students. We learnt much about how to develop metacognitive awareness in our students and became more metacognitive ourselves. We developed a strong sense of commitment to supporting the developing skills of others by sharing our experiences of the research process. We became more aware of our professional growth, about how threatening growth can be and how hard it can be to manage.

We now sit between the two worlds, in a place where as teacher-researchers we can access the worlds of teachers and academics. Throughout our journey we have experienced the pleasure that personal and professional growth gives, as well as the dilemma of not knowing where we 'fit in'. We have moved on and cannot be comfortable in the way we once were, but with the gains come some losses.

We hold on to the thought that tall poppies are terrific—they have grown and developed from small beginnings. We hope that where only a small number of poppies stand tall today, tomorrow there will be a whole patch: '*Surely the winds couldn't knock down a whole bunch of poppies.*'

REFERENCES

Baird, J.R. and Mitchell, I.J. (1986). *Improving the Quality of Teaching and Learning: An Australian Case Study—the PEEL Project.* Melbourne: Monash University.

Baird, J.R. and Northfield, J.R. (1992). *Learning from the PEEL Experience.* Melbourne: Monash University.

Flack, J., Osler, J. and Mitchell, I. (1995). Mapping the Swamp. *Reflect—The Journal of Reflection in Learning and Teaching*, 1 (1), 11–19.

Flack, J. and Osler, J. (2000). We're Teachers, We're Researchers, We're Proud of It! *Australian Educational Researcher*, 26 (3), 89–104.

Osler, J. and Flack, J. (2000). Learning Together—Teachers and Students Sharing the Classroom. Unpublished Classroom Research Project. Melbourne: Monash University.

Loughran, J.J. (1999). Professional Development for Teachers: A Growing Concern. *The Journal of In-Service Education*, 25 (2), 261–72.

PART 5

Conclusion

13

Learning from teacher research for teacher research

Ian Mitchell

INTRODUCTION

In this chapter I address three questions. What can we learn about:

- teacher research;
- promoting quality learning; and,
- effectively communicating the wisdom from teacher research to other teachers?

When looking for general themes in the preceding chapters, it is worth remembering that PAVOT did not mandate any particular research questions and the projects varied in many ways. The only cohering factors were shared concerns about passive learning and a common interest in improving how students learned.

WHAT CAN WE LEARN ABOUT TEACHER RESEARCH?

Some features of the process

Motivation and research questions

For all the projects, improving the teachers' classrooms was an important goal of the research. Generating and documenting knowledge for others was, at least initially, a side benefit. This has carried a cost for us: writing has sometimes been one demand too many. Teachers, whose working life does not encourage or reward writing, have achieved their main goal if, by doing the research, their classroom is better and they understand their practice better—sharing with a wider audience provides few extra rewards. Not all of the projects we have supported through PAVOT have been reported.

When PAVOT began in 1994, we expected that the teachers would choose small, manageable areas to research. This has not been the case. All of the teachers wanted to see significant change in how their students learned (an attractive goal for most teachers), but to do this they have had to track large chunks of classroom life. This reflects the complex, interconnected nature of both learning and teaching. Even those who began with a focus on one aspect of learning soon found that this pulled in many other aspects of classroom practice.

Structure and support

One of the important principles in both PEEL and PAVOT is that teachers have a sense of ownership and control of their research. This was easy for the teachers who investigated only their own classrooms. It was a more complex issue in the projects that involved other teachers. The work of a teacher-researcher can easily threaten colleagues. If possible, projects that impact on colleagues should be structured to give them a sense of shared ownership with options for different starting points and different levels of involvement.

A teacher-research project does not require more than one teacher in the team, but it is helpful to have colleagues involved. The process can be lonely and several chapters testify to the value of, and support gained by, regular, often informal brainstorming and sharing with other on-site colleagues. For all the projects, the collaborative atmosphere at the regular PAVOT meetings was essential. These involved the teachers sharing ideas and experiences with university-based colleagues as well as with members of (usually) two other teams. At these meetings, the academics commonly provided advice, but so did the teachers—teams advised each other. Often our most important role was one of affirmation: building the teachers' confidence that others could learn from their experiences.

Developments over time

Cochran-Smith and Lytle (1999) reported the prominence of teacher research in professional development. Among other things, PEEL provides a structure for long-term professional development, but we have found that, as teachers develop, they become ready and interested to take on new types of roles. The long-term involvement of most of the teachers in PEEL means that their starting points, and hence what they were able to achieve, were different—often very different from what they would have been without this experience. This means that many of the chapters provide windows into what can happen, at both the individual and the school level, in a project that has very long timelines.

Our experiences with the types of research goals that attract PEEL teachers are that long timelines are often essential. One reason for this is that achieving significant change in what students do and believe about learning requires the prior development and refinement of a considerable body of new classroom practice. This includes the development of both the ideas and the teachers' skill and experience in implementing them. This takes time, often years. In Chapter 1, John referred to the importance of the internal literature of PEEL, built up over sixteen years of teachers working to improve how students learn. This literature was important for many of the teachers, but so was their lived experience with these ideas. Timelines of numbers of years need not, however, be onerous for teacher-researchers—they commonly experience rewards and benefits at all stages of the journey.

Rigour

Cochran-Smith and Lytle (1999) describe a 'methods critique' of teacher research: that it is no different from other interpretive research, but weakened by the researcher being a participant and too lacking in rigour and objectivity to be useful. As many of the chapters show, teacher research is often messy and non-linear, with progress not obvious for long periods of time and with some of the most important outcomes occurring in directions different from (albeit consistent with) the original goals. One reason for this messiness is the complex, interconnected and broadly focused nature of the projects. A second reason is that formal data collection must be accommodated around the teachers' primary responsibilities for teaching their classes. This means that it is sometimes not as systematic and complete as the teacher would like; however, this weakness in data collection is often compensated for by advantages (discussed later) that flow from the researcher being the teacher and being always present. Unpicking rich practice is not simple and practice commonly precedes understanding in teacher research. Teachers commonly need to try new approaches, test the boundaries of what seems possible, and often achieve change before they can develop clear understandings of what they are doing, what they are achieving and why.

Unlike much interpretive research, teacher-researchers do not set out on studies of 'what is' in their classrooms; rather, they set out to change them. This means that all opportunities for improving practice are immediately taken. Taking on a research role often reveals unsuspected deficiencies in learning. Professional ethics and values mean that teachers will immediately act on their new insights and change practice to improve learning. An interpretive researcher studying 'what is' may prefer to confirm over repeated lessons (for example) a student misinterpretation of part of a new curriculum package. In one sense, this will yield stronger data than that which might emerge from a teacher-researcher who takes immediate action to improve the package. However, a compensating strength is that the links between insight and tested consequences for practice, so often missing in the literature, are almost a guaranteed outcome.

Effects of doing research on teacher-researchers

Willingness to take risks
Attempting substantial change in how classrooms or schools operate usually seems very risky. Teacher-researchers are choosing to be learners, accepting a period of deskilling and entering unknown territory. They have to carry the consequences in their classrooms and with their colleagues for the rest of the year if things go badly. A consistent message from PEEL teachers is that they have learnt that the risks are less than they seem. When students are given more responsibility and control (and hence a greater ability to cause lessons to fail), they respond appropriately and positively. Experienced teacher-researchers become the high risk-takers we need to develop innovative practice.

Their ability to generalise and articulate their practice
Loughran et al. (2000) set out to capture the pedagogical content knowledge of Science teachers; they report considerable difficulty in accessing this knowledge, with teachers finding it difficult to describe what they believe they do well. The literature contains many references to teacher knowledge, but is almost empty of rich descriptions of that knowledge.

As Rosemary (Chapter 10) and Jill and Jo (Chapter 12) reported, an important impact of several years of teacher research is a greatly enhanced ability to recognise, generalise and articulate the important features of their practice. The teachers both develop and borrow new frames that help them make new sense of what was previously craft knowledge (Grimmet and Mackinnon, 1992). This growth does not come quickly; it involves new ways of knowing (Cochran-Smith and Lytle, 1999)—new ways of thinking and talking about practice. This is an area where collaboration with academics can be very helpful, provided both groups recognise that they bring different and equally valuable expertise and ways of thinking to the partnership—that each has much to learn from the other.

Their perceptions of their role
A recurring feature of every PAVOT project has been the teachers' initial reluctance to accept that they have interesting and often

important things to say to the wider world of education. Gillian (Chapter 9) reports how, well after she started, she came to believe that she had something to say to others. Jill and Jo (Chapter 12) made this a major theme of their chapter. The fact that they chose to do this, rather than focus on their wealth of insight into improving the learning of young students (e.g. Flack, Osler and Mitchell, 1995), is in itself evidence of how long their journey has been.

Mandi and Pippa (Chapter 11) provide another example of a reconceptualising of role: they had assumed initially that the literature would provide them with at least part of what they needed. They soon realised that there was a whole category of knowledge that only teacher-researchers such as they could generate.

Deborah (Chapter 3) had a different shift in relation to the literature. Part of her research (collecting views on homework) was more similar than most of the other projects to what a non-teacher-researcher might do and, after she began to gather data systematically, she recognised that there was likely to be useful research published in this area. Our experience, however, has been that few of the PAVOT teams have developed an interest in the traditional literature—it offers too low a frequency of useful articles for busy teachers whose prime concern is improving their own classroom. I discuss later the sorts of evidence that are important to teacher-researchers, but I comment here that many of the teachers joined PAVOT with a fairly traditional and narrow view of research. They also had little respect for the authority of their own voices (Munby and Russell, 1994). Although critical incidents from their classrooms (for example) would be convincing to them, it generally took time for them to accept that accounts of these incidents could be credible evidence for others.

The journey is irreversible
The PAVOT teachers' research changed their classroom practice in ways that were important and permanent. Even though teaching in some ways becomes more demanding, with higher standards for a 'good' lesson, there is no going back. As one becomes sensitive to hitherto unrecognised passive learning, one can never ignore it.

The journey of engaging in teacher research is also, to some degree, a one-way exercise. Initially, we assumed that teachers would take on more formal research for perhaps a year or two and then stop. This often happened, but for many teachers the process was so enjoyable and the changes in their perceptions of their role in education so profound that they could not go back. This has been enormously valuable—as teachers spend more years engaged in teacher research, they tackle more sophisticated challenges and share these in more sophisticated ways.

Types of outcomes

As John stated in Chapter 1, the teachers looked into their classrooms in different ways, seeking data that shed new light on their teaching. The types of things they found can be placed in three groups.

Challenges to common practice and reconceptions of what is possible
Many of the chapters raise important—sometimes fundamental—challenges to practices that are common in schools. Rosemary (Chapter 10) challenged much conventional Mathematics teaching, Jo and David (Chapter 7) challenged the assessment practices at their school, Mandi and Pippa (Chapter 11) brought out the phoniness of much learning in Science, Deborah (Chapter 3) challenged the whole basis of homework for younger students. On reading their work, it is hard to avoid the conclusion that these teachers are targeting issues that should matter to schools and systems.

Part of the power of these challenges to existing practice is that many of them provide new visions of what is possible. All of the authors took significant risks at various times, yet they consistently found that the risks were worth taking. By sharing their personal and contextualised accounts, they have shown that substantial change is possible in real classrooms.

Greater understandings of student learning and of student change
One reason for the continuation of PEEL has been that teachers find considerable personal value in better understanding the learning that is, and is not, occurring in their classes. Important parts of this new knowledge are greater understandings of barriers to good learning

generally and to the learning of a particular area of content. Shulman (1987) included this latter knowledge in his description of peda-gogical content knowledge that he said was held by all or most experienced teachers. Our experiences suggest that this sort of knowledge becomes enormously more sophisticated after a few years of teacher research in ways that reflect much greater insight into both learning and change. This includes insights into limitations on the rate of change, important features of change and how to promote change. This type of knowledge, which is uncommon in the literature, is as important a part of the 'how to' understandings as the knowledge of new practices.

Such insights form one basis for the challenges to existing practice discussed above. PEEL teachers consistently have found that many apparently successful lessons involve far less thinking, awareness of purpose and growth of understanding than teachers imagine.

The insights are not all negative: Rosemary (Chapter 10) and Pia (Chapter 6), who were testing the limits of how fast they could change student learning, found that their students were, to some degree, unaware of how far they had come.

Apart from the contribution to our general assertions about passive learning, an important value of the individual insights in this area is for the teachers themselves. These new understandings of what is happening in their classrooms are very powerful sources of motivation to persist in the often risky and tiring process of developing, testing and refining new approaches. The teachers shift from a search for simple answers to complex problems to seeing ideas for new practice in terms of their possibilities for further elaboration and development (Loughran, 1999).

Development of new practices

Teacher-researchers want to improve their classrooms and want to extend their understandings of how to achieve this. As Mandi and Pippa (Chapter 11) noted, important aspects of the knowledge that they needed was absent from the literature. All of the teachers devel-oped new, innovative practice that flowed from and was linked to their greater understandings of learning and change. Documenting this wisdom was not a goal of this book and it is more often referred or

alluded to than detailed. However, building this practically sophisticated knowledge has been very important for each researcher. The
PEEL CD-ROM (Mitchell, Mitchell and McKinnon, 2001) contains a
database of over 700 ideas developed by PEEL teachers. As discussed
earlier, good teacher research commonly results in new classroom
knowledge that provides the 'so what' and 'how do you use these
findings' aspects of research that are so important for teachers.
Without this sort of knowledge, the prospects of research findings—
however valuable and salient to classrooms—actually influencing
practice is small.

The evidence for new knowledge that teachers found convincing

Weaknesses in the data that teacher-researchers report is part of the
'methods critique' (Cochran-Smith and Lytle, 1999). As John said in
Chapter 1, these teachers were concerned about evidence, but their
first interest was evidence that was convincing to them when making
judgments about their attempts to improve their own classroom
practice. Evidence for teacher and academic readers was important,
but was less important. Given these priorities, it is worth looking at
the types of evidence that they regarded as personally convincing.
It is then worth asking how convincing they are to a reader and what,
if any, further evidence is needed.

Critical incidents were often very significant and descriptions of
these are important in several chapters. Jill and Jo (Chapter 12)
systematically collected them. Critical incidents for Kerry and Judie
(Chapter 2) and Deborah (Chapter 3) convinced them of the need
for change; the incident in Lyn's case (Chapter 5) convinced her that
change was possible. Several incidents confirmed to the teachers
that change had occurred. Classroom change is evolutionary and,
although critical incidents are commonly unexpected (hence their
power for the teacher), they rarely—if ever—reflect a sudden quan-
tum advance. Instead, as Pia's incident (Chapter 6) illustrates, they
reveal change (usually in students' conceptions of and/or attitudes to
learning) that had been occurring without being obvious.

The validity and power of critical incidents as a form of evidence must, to a large degree, lie with the reader. It is the teacher's job to describe incidents in a way that is convincing, sensitive to the multi-faceted complexity of classrooms and demonstrates that they are as willing to share failures and doubts as they are to report successes.

Another, related, type of evidence that was convincing to the teachers was gradual but persistent changes in students' classroom behaviours (such as continual displays of good learning behaviours). This knowledge has two bases. One is the teacher's past experience with similar groups of (say) Year 8 English students. The other is the teacher's knowledge of what was and was not a significant change for a particular class or individual. Once again, this type of data is strengthened by reports of difficulties and aspects that were not positive. Its received validity will also be strengthened by the reader's experience and familiarity with the teacher's context.

Not surprisingly, these two types of data often provide the strong-est evidence for the teacher. However, in almost all cases, the teachers wanted to triangulate these data with that from other sources such as surveys, interviews, retention rates or the before/after comparison of how Lyn's students drew a learner (Chapter 5).

In summary, whilst individual projects varied, it is reasonable to say that what mattered most to these teachers was aspects of what their students did during class time. This, after all, is the data they are best placed to collect (they are always there) and interpret (they know their class contexts). They report these classroom behaviours as vignettes and cases, but they often need persuading that these will be convincing to others.

Some strengths and unique features of teacher research

I referred earlier to the inevitable messiness of the research that teachers can conduct while teaching full-time. However, there are compensating advantages. One is that it is easier to collect data over the long periods of time that are needed to research substantial changes to classroom practice. In addition, the teacher is always there and hence is in a position to capture all the unexpected incidents that are so often important data.

Huberman (1996) criticised teacher research because of the difficulty of researching events in which one is a player. This overlooks one important issue—teacher-research attempts to improve classrooms. The complexity of classrooms means that no significant change to practice can be neatly planned in advance. A teacher-researcher can react to unexpected events with immediate changes to the new practice—often the reaction *must* be immediate. A teacher who is working with (or for) an outside researcher is likely to feel a need to consult first and the moment will be lost.

What sorts of problems can teacher-researchers best tackle?

Teachers are not the only people suited to conducting research in classrooms. For reasons given earlier, they may not be best placed, for example, to conduct a detailed, narrowly focused study of one particular aspect of classroom practice nor a study of what is occurring that involves leaving the teaching unchanged. Studies that require continuous observation of what individual groups of students do in the classroom are also not easily undertaken by the person who is conducting the lesson.

There are areas, however, where teachers are best placed to conduct the research. One is tackling problems that are long-term and require the development of considerable classroom wisdom. A second is when an intervention involves significant risk for the teacher and/or where the intervention requires changes to many aspects of the classroom practice: a series of unsuccessful lessons can have serious long-term costs for teachers and they are unlikely to persist with refining and retrying a radical new approach owned by someone else. A third is research that focuses on issues of student dissatisfaction and disengagement. Here the teacher often needs to be very reactive to events and hence, as discussed earlier, needs to be in charge of the intervention.

WHAT HAVE WE LEARNT ABOUT PROMOTING QUALITY LEARNING?

PEEL teachers have spent sixteen years researching and developing ways of improving the quality of student learning. This is a major theme of most chapters, but drawing together all that we know and have learnt in this area was not a purpose of this book. To make no comment on what is PEEL's principal goal would decontextualise and diminish the work of the teachers, but in this section I restrict myself to relatively brief comments on what emerges from these chapters. More comprehensive accounts of the work of PEEL can be found in Baird and Northfield (1995), Baird and Mitchell (1997) and Mitchell, Mitchell and McKinnon (2001).

Features of good learning

There are a number of features of what we regard as quality in student learning that flow across the chapters. This strengthens the claims of improvement made by each individual author. Good learning behaviours were common and they significantly affected how the classrooms operated. There were high levels of student interest, intellectual engagement and on-task behaviour. There were increases in students' confidence, intellectual self-esteem and willingness to take risks. The students were more willing and able to take some responsibility for aspects of what they did in class. Finally, there were increases in the levels of both student–student and student–teacher collaboration. Both the nature and the extent of these changes were non-trivial, and they offer substantial intrinsic rewards to teachers. They are consistent with a long history of educational writings about improving classrooms—for example, Dewey (1933) and Holt (1969).

Features of student change

Changing how students learn is not simple. One reason for this is that it requires changes in students' beliefs about what are proper, appropriate and possible behaviours for students and teachers. One interesting aspect of this issue was the sometimes marked difference between what the students actually did—the (positive) ways they were prepared to learn—and the less positive comments about the teaching and/or learning that they made with hindsight at a later date. This does highlight the need for regular overt debriefing with students at the time about what is happening, and why, in order to maximise their metacognitive awareness of the changes in their learning.

These points provide reasons why quality learning requires learners' consent (Loughran and Northfield, 1996). Teachers can mandate low-level busy-work and completion of routine tasks, but they cannot mandate high-quality (and high-risk) learning behaviours such as offering and defending alternative explanations. Many of the chapters show that student change can only be gradual and evolution-ary. This, however, does not mean that it cannot be very substantial.

Features of the teaching

Collectively, the chapters provide good evidence that the twelve principles of teaching for quality learning (Table 1.3) do describe important features of the teaching of PEEL teachers. All of the principles are prominent in a number of chapters and every chapter reflects many of the principles.

Each principle can be enacted in a range of ways. Sharing intellec-tual control—a feature of every teacher's practice—variously involved starting from students' ideas, promoting and using students' ques-tions, responding to students' suggestions, concerns or criticisms, giving students genuine choices or giving students veto over what was to be done. One outcome of this was to promote student activity rather than passivity—but activity where the students were often initiators or collaborators with the teacher. Associated with this prin-ciple was the extent to which the teachers listened to their students and were willing to be seen by their students as learners.

We believe that many of these twelve principles are present (albeit often tacitly) in the practice of large numbers of good teachers who are not in PEEL (although a much smaller number of teachers would enact many of them). However, we suggest that principles 9 (Use teaching procedures that are designed to promote specific aspects of quality learning) and 11 (Regularly raise students' awareness of the nature of components of quality learning) are uncommon outside PEEL classrooms. Many of these chapters describe teachers deliberately setting out to promote aspects of quality learning such as linking different topics or retrieving existing conceptions. This is a result of the teachers' enhanced understandings of learning. Many more describe systematic efforts to promote a metacognitive awareness of learning.

The overall effect of the above changes was that all of the classrooms moved away from a focus on classroom management and from a focus on tasks. They moved to a focus on the big ideas behind the tasks (principle 10), on the quality of how the students were learning and to a consistent expectation that the students could and would engage in activities that required high-order thinking and high levels of intellectual engagement and awareness of purpose.

COMMUNICATING TEACHER RESEARCH TO OTHER TEACHERS

Academics commonly search for generalisable findings that will communicate to a wide audience. Teacher-researchers are more interested, at least initially, in finding what may appear to be context-specific solutions to problems in their own classrooms. We have found, however, that much of the wisdom that teacher-researchers generate can generalise across many contexts (Mitchell and Mitchell, 2001), and so should be communicated to other teachers. For several reasons, this is not easy to do. One reason for this difficulty is that the main reason for doing it is to stimulate teacher readers to improve their own practice. Yet practice is not easily changed by words on paper.

One aspect of the problem is that the long journeys of teacher-researchers like Jill and Jo (Chapter 12) and Rosemary (Chapter 10) leave them with practice that is well in advance of the norm. In addition to being long, the journey is also personal in terms of the particular ways they apply more general principles. For both of these reasons, long-term teacher-researchers have no interest in telling other teachers to suddenly 'be like them'. Jill and Jo (Chapter 12) talked about the real problems they have faced in becoming somewhat disconnected from their colleagues. A related aspect of this issue is that, in some important ways, the journey is experiential—some parts of the story cannot just be told, they must also be experienced.

There appear to be four areas where some personal experience is important, if not essential. One is to personally experience the failure of apparently successful teaching. A second is the extent to which risks usually pay off—one has to take a risk of one's own. A third is to experience lessons that demonstrate what is possible in one's own classroom in terms of student engagement in quality learning. The fourth is to experience the importance and value of developing one's own variations and extensions of other people's ideas; to shift from a search for recipes that can be used intact to more generic ideas that must be customised to one's particular context. Communicative teacher research needs to provide teachers with opportunities to gain all four types of experience.

Different teacher readers are at different stages of their own journeys and so have different interests and needs. What is an attractive idea for one reader is intimidating to another. Lyn, after several years in PEEL, was very willing to adopt Gillian's ideas of the L Files, but this would not be an attractive entry point for a teacher who had never heard of the list of good learning behaviours. Ideally, communications of teacher research should suggest different entry points for different readers.

Teachers want to see classrooms via credible, contextually rich accounts of specific incidents. These need to be combined with commentaries—ways of framing the problem—that provide teachers with ways into either experiencing the problem (e.g. ways of uncovering students' alternative conceptions in Science) or into starting to do something about it. The accounts need to provide advice and ideas that will allow readers to experiment at different levels of risk. Accounts that gloss over difficulties and present stories of unmitigated triumph are *unlikely* to be credible to teachers. Moreover, the difficulties and less successful aspects can often represent interesting consequential problems for readers to tackle.

Communicating teacher research in accessible and useful ways to other teachers involves some very different issues from those associated with communicating the same research to academics. The nature of teachers' work and teachers' interests and needs means, for example, that communicating research to teachers cannot and should not be disconnected from issues of professional development.

CONCLUDING COMMENTS

There is an increasing interest in teacher research, but for a number of reasons it is not yet occupying an important place in the research literature. We believe that there are important questions and important kinds of knowledge that can be addressed and generated only by research by teachers. However, it is not proving simple to create the climate, conditions and structures that allow teacher research to make the sorts of contributions that Stenhouse (1975) argued for so long ago.

Tackling this problem requires greater understanding (and more research) in a number of areas, two of which have been a focus of this chapter. The first is the nature of teacher research: how it proceeds, its strengths, unique characteristics and limitations and the sorts of conditions that support and sustain it. Teacher research will be more successful if it focuses on what it does well and where it can make unique and needed contributions. We also need more research into the nature of the professional knowledge of teachers generally, and of teachers who have had varying levels of experience in research. One aspect of this issue is the sorts of data and knowledge claims that these different groups of teachers find convincing. If we wish to promote an education culture where teachers are more aware of, and articulate about, their professional knowledge, and where they regularly reflect on, refine and extend their professional knowledge, then we need to know more about how teachers build and store professional knowledge in the complex world of classroom practice.

Finally, there is the area of communicating the findings of teacher-researchers to other groups in education. The issues associated with communicating teacher research to academics are obviously different from those associated with communicating to teachers. Academics are expected to read and, at least in part, read to expand their professional knowledge. Teacher research is a separate genre that generates important (and currently scarce) kinds of knowledge. Criteria for quality in teacher research should be strongly influenced by the criteria and features that teacher-researchers find important and convincing, rather than criteria that are transposed from different fields of research.

REFERENCES

Baird, J.R. and Mitchell, I.J. (eds) (1997). *Improving the Quality of Teaching and Learning*. Melbourne: PEEL Publishing.

Baird, J.R. and Northfield, J.R. (eds) (1995). *Learning from the PEEL Experience*. Melbourne: PEEL Publishing.

Cochran-Smith, M. and Lytle, S.L. (1999). The Teacher Research Movement: A Decade Later. *Educational Researcher 28* (7), 15–25.

Dewey, J. (1933). *How We Think*. New York: Heath & Co.

Flack, J., Osler, J. and Mitchell, I.J. (1995). Mapping the Swamp: A Case Study of Reflective Practice. *Reflect 1* (1), 11–19.

Grimmet, P.P. and Mackinnon, A.M. (1992). Craft Knowledge and the Education of Teachers. *Review of Educational Research 18*, 385–456.

Holt, J. (1969). *How Children Fail*. Harmondsworth: Penguin.

Huberman, M. (1996). Focus on Research Moving Mainstream: Taking a Closer Look at Teacher Research. *Language Arts 73* (2), 124–40.

Loughran, J.J. (1999). Professional Development for Teachers: A Growing Concern. *The Journal of In-Service Education 25* (2), 261–72.

Loughran, J.J., Gunstone, R.F., Berry, A., Milroy, P. and Mulhall, P. (2000). *Science Cases in Action: Developing an Understanding of Science Teachers' Pedagogical Content Knowledge*. New Orleans: National Association for Research in Science Teaching.

Loughran, J.J. and Northfield, J.R. (1996). *Opening the Classroom Door: Teacher, Researcher, Learner*. London: Falmer Press.

Mitchell, I.J. and Mitchell, J.A. (2001). Constructing and Sharing Generalizable Statements of Teacher Knowledge from Context-specific Accounts of Innovative Practice. Seattle: Annual

Conference of the American Educational Research Association.

Mitchell, I.J., Mitchell, J. and McKinnon. R. (2001). *PEEL in Practice: 700 Ideas for Quality Teaching* (CD-ROM). Melbourne: PEEL Publishing.

Munby, H. and Russell, T. (1994). The Authority of Experience in Learning to Teach: Messages from a Physics Methods Class. *Journal of Teacher Education 45* (2), 85–95.

Shulman, L.S. (1987). Knowledge and Teaching: Foundations of the New Reform. *Harvard Educational Review 57* (1), 1–22.

Stenhouse, L. (1975). *An Introduction to Curriculum Reasearch and Development*. London: Heinemann.

Index